THE MORNING STAR

God's gift for daily living

Denise Rinker Adler
edited by Rosalind Rinker

A Key-Word Book
WORD BOOKS, Publisher
Waco, Texas

A KEY-WORD BOOK

Published by Pillar Books for Word Books, Publisher

THE MORNING STAR

Copyright © 1974 by Rosalind Rinker.
All rights reserved.
No part of this book may be reproduced in any form,
except for brief quotations in reviews,
without the written permission of publisher and author.

First Key-Word Book edition—July 1976
Library of Congress catalog card number: 74-82652.
ISBN # 0-87680-862-3
Printed in the United States of America.

Quotations from the Revised Standard Version of the Bible (RSV), copyright 1946, 1952, © 1971, 1973 by the Division of Christian Education of the National Council of the Churches of Christ in the U.S.A., are used by permission.

Quotations from *The New English Bible* (NEB), © The Delegates of the Oxford University Press and The Syndics of the Cambridge University Press, 1961, 1970, are used by permission.

Quotations from the Today's English Version of the New Testament (TEV), copyright © American Bible Society 1966, are used by permission.

Quotations from *The Living Bible, Paraphrased* (LB), © 1971 by Tyndale House Publishers, Wheaton, Illinois, are used by permission.

Quotations from J. B. Phillips, *The New Testament in Modern English,* published by Macmillan Co., are © 1958, 1960, 1972 by J. B. Phillips.

Quotations marked *Amplified* are from *The Amplified Bible,* © 1965 by Zondervan Publishing House.

Quotations from the Berkeley Version of the Bible are copyright 1945, 1959 by Zondervan Publishing House.

Quotations marked ASV are from the American Standard Version of the Bible, copyright 1901 by Thomas Nelson & Sons.

Quotations marked KJV are from the King James or Authorized Version of the Bible.

Quotations marked KJ II are from the King James Version of the Bible, revised edition, © Jay P. Green, 1971, Associated Publishers and Authors, Byron Center, Michigan.

First Month

244
RIN

DAY 1

Read Psalm 104.

My meditation of him shall be sweet: I will be glad in the Lord.

Psalm 104:34, KJV.

What does meditation mean to you? How do you meditate? The dictionary definition is: to reflect on, or muse over, to engage in contemplation or reflection.

To me, meditation means to be very quiet. To keep my hands and my feet quiet. To be in a room away from noise for at least fifteen to twenty minutes. To remain quiet, with "open listening" in the presence of my Father God who loves me. To let thoughts about Him well up in my heart. To worship Him in the beauty of holiness. (This is not a problem-solving time.)

What does meditation do for me? It quiets and rests my physical body. It takes away the anxious fretting spirit and in its place puts confidence. It shows me to whom I belong. It relaxes me spiritually and physically. It helps me get into a receptive mood. It helps me know which way I am going.

"Meditation" makes me sensitive first to my own needs and then to the needs of others. I call it "transforming meditation" (T.M.) because it has power to change me. I am better able to understand myself, I am able to be glad and to rejoice in spite of hard things. I find myself wanting to continue and looking forward to the next time of T.M.

The world today uses the term "transcendental meditation" (T.M.), but there is no loving Father in it, unless you turn your face towards Him. Let's call it *"transforming* meditation" because, in His Presence, we are changed into His likeness. We absorb His love and thus become loving. We absorb His restoring power, His comfort and His peace. He is always ready to walk with us in paths of righteousness for His Name's sake.

Let us who are called by His Name, practice the art of open listening, the art of meditation.

DAY 2

Read Psalm 19.

*The heavens are telling the glory of God;
and the firmament proclaims his handiwork.*
                Psalm 19:1, RSV.

Women are ordinary folk, busy in a world of home and work. Some of us are bounded on the north by a kitchen sink and stove, on the east by an ironing board, on the west by children at play, and on the north with washing and mending. We can't spend long hours praying on our knees or contemplating or reading Christian books. Many times when we sit down, we fall asleep because we are too tired to think about anything. The outdoor world around us, God's handiwork, is ignored because we are too tired.

Our boundaries need not limit us from serving Christ. And we must learn to see God in everything and praise Him for His goodness, or we shall shrivel, dry up and blow away as the wind blows the chaff. Unless we lift our eyes and see the heavens telling God's glory in the sunrise and the sunset and the expanse of stars, the monotony of children and housework will easily make life meaningless.

There are three things we can do to help ourselves.

1. Make a deliberate point of seeing the green growing things God has made, as well as the beauty in the morning and evening skies. Once I planted petunias in a box outside my kitchen window. Most of them died, but there was one red and white striped one that flourished. Every time I looked at it, it made my day. I talked to it and to God. "Thank you, Lord, for that nice fat petunia. It's gorgeous and you made it for my enjoyment. It stands perfectly still, it's not going any place, nor doing anything except growing and blooming. Lord, make me like that fat petunia, staying put, doing my own thing and giving your beauty to others."

2. See the hand of God in everything, right there in the kitchen, the sewing room, the nursery. Brother Lawrence, in his little classic, *The Practice of the Pres-*

ence of God, tells us that God was just as real to him in the kitchen among the pots and pans as when he was kneeling in the sanctuary receiving the sacrament. He could see God's glory as he worked in the kitchen.

3. Set aside half an hour for a Quiet Time daily. Edwin Lewis says, "We must find the Presence through the quiet hour if we are to keep it through the noisy hour." When we take time and shut ourselves away from the world and pray to our Father in secret, He will reward us openly with His presence.

DAY 3

Read Luke 6:27–38.

"Give, and it will be given to you; good measure, pressed down, shaken together, running over."

Luke 6:38, RSV.

"What you give keeps, and what you keep spoils" is an old proverb.

"It is more blessed to give than to receive," Jesus told us (Acts 20:35 KJV).

If you give, "God shall supply all your need according to his riches in glory" (Phil. 4:19, KJV).

There are three things I have learned from my own personal giving. 1. God is the source of everything I need in this life. In Him dwells every perfect thing, so in all things I am enriched by him (James 1:17; 1 Cor. 1:5). 2. I give Him my very best, not second best; I give Him myself and all that I have—completely and unreservedly, and He gives me His very best. 3. After I have given, I expect His blessing because He promised and I have a right to expect a miracle to happen.

It works like this for me: I feel the Lord wants me to give a tithe out of my grocery and household money. My husband has given the tithe from his salary, but I feel the need of doing this myself. I want the special blessing God has promised. As I pray about this, certain needs and certain people are brought to my mind.

I thank the Lord that I am able to do this, and I remind the Lord that He has all of me and not just my few dollars. Then I look for the special blessing He has promised to give to me or to the person who has received the money. It never fails to happen.

Once you have experienced this process, you will always be a giver, for God always outgives you as you become a source of blessing. Read Luke 6:38 again. This time make it personal: "Denise (your name), you give to Me out of what you have, and I will give you good measure, pressed down and running over."

DAY 4

Read Luke 10:25–37.

You shall love . . . your neighbor as yourself.

Luke 10:27, KJ II.

Jesus told us in this second of the two great commandments, that we were first to love ourselves and then it would be possible for us to love our neighbors. Implied in this statement is the truth that it is good for us to love ourselves, to esteem ourselves highly.

The fact is, however, that more people think too little of themselves than too much. It is easier to feel unimportant than important. More of us sin in lowering ourselves in our own estimation, than in being conceited and proud. When we minimize and underestimate ourselves, we have lost sight of our own value.

When I came to know God's personal love for me, a great transformation started in my life. I began to learn to love and respect myself, and then I found I could love my neighbor. I was able to give myself to God and to people in a way I could not do before.

Some of us must learn to love ourselves through the process of conversion. John Gaynor Banks, in *Healing Everywhere* (p. 25), defines conversion as "that process gradual or sudden, by which a soul, previously divided and consciously wrong, inferior, and unhappy, becomes unified and consciously right, superior and happy."

There is a sense in which we define conversion as "being born into" God's family, once and for all. At the same time, the kind of conversion defined in the last paragraph takes in all of us and is continually necessary, for as life's patterns ebb and flow around us, we are in need of periodic times of change, of renewal, of being turned from our own way to God's way.

"You shall love . . . your neighbor as yourself."

DAY 5

Read Luke 11:1–13.

Lord, teach us to pray, as John also taught his disciples.

Luke 11:1, KJV.

The only subject on record for which the disciples requested teaching was prayer. Apparently the prayer life and practices of Jesus and the power which accompanied His life, as well as the life of John the Baptist, made a deep impression on them. They saw that prayer had value; it had results that could be measured.

In my own life, there are three areas in which prayer produces change.

First, my mind is quickened. I can understand the things of the Spirit more easily and readily.

Second, my affections are released toward the entire world and more especially toward the persons I am praying for. I am giving love to them through prayer.

Third, my imagination is kindled. I find I can form pictures in my mind of what I am reading from the Bible. I can picture the hands of Jesus touching me. I can imagine something of what heaven is going to be like, and the welcome awaiting me there. I find joy in using my imagination.

We learn to pray by praying. Start with simple, short, honest sentences, and your thoughts will be guided by the Spirit. For the Holy Spirit is your teacher today. Wherever He leads your thoughts, turn them into prayers—and always with thanksgiving.

DAY 6

Read Luke 11:1–4.

Our Father, who art in heaven . . .
     Luke 11:2, KJ II.

Jesus' teaching was autobiographical, springing fresh from his own daily prayer life. In answering the disciples' request, "Teach us to pray," He taught them the words of what we now call The Lord's Prayer.

Jesus in this prayer gives us the principles which underlie the true relationship between God and man. Hallowing the name of the Father is adoration. Praying for God's will to be done opens our spirits so that we may understand God's purposes. Essentially we have to adjust and relate ourselves to God and his purposes rather than have him adjust to us.

When we pray, "Our Father, who art in heaven, hallowed be thy name," our attention is called to the glory, majesty, and perfection of God. If we meditate on these attributes of God, our reaction is to fall on our knees in adoration and reverence. Thinking about Him lifts us out of ourselves and prepares us for communication with Him.

After this act of worship, we are ready to ask and to receive. *Give us our daily bread. Forgive us and help us to forgive others . . . and don't allow us to be tempted beyond our powers to resist.*

Thus is the will of God done on earth, and thus does His will become ours—in the acts of receiving and in the acts of giving.

"Thy will be done, as in heaven, so in earth."

DAY 7

Read Luke 18:35–43.

He asked him, "What do you want me to do for you?" He said, "Lord, let me receive my sight."   Luke 18:41, RSV.

The Lord Jesus is saying to you, "What do you want me to do for you today?" Your answer could be, "Just bless me, Lord, and my husband and my son and my daughter." And then you could add, "if it be Thy will," just to make it sound right and not selfish.

With an indefinite prayer like this, how can you expect an answer? In the reading for today, a specific person asked Jesus for a definite thing. And he received a definite answer.

The blind beggar at Jericho (he is called Bartimaeus in Mark 10), on hearing that Jesus was passing by, began to cry out for mercy. (It is good to cry for mercy, but according to this account, it is not definite enough.) The people in the crowd around rebuked him for making such a disturbance, but that made him shout out all the louder, "Jesus, thou Son of David, have mercy on me."

Jesus heard him, stopped, and called for him to come. "What do you want me to do for you?" He asked.

"Lord, I want my sight restored," the blind man answered.

Jesus replied, "Receive your sight; your faith has made you well."

And immediately he received his sight.

What did he do next? He followed Jesus, giving glory to God.

Bartimaeus made a definite, specific request and got the same kind of an answer. Do you suppose he made an indefinite request the next time he was faced with a need? He knew just whom to go to and how to ask.

How did the answer he received affect others? The last part of the Scripture tells us. "And all the people, when they saw it, gave praise unto God."

"Glory to God in the highest!"

DAY 8

Read 2 Corinthians 10:1-9.

> *It is true that I am an ordinary, weak human being, but I don't use human plans and methods to win my battles.*
> 2 Corinthians 10:3, LB.

I once felt trapped by my negative feelings—that I was helpless, that feelings couldn't be changed, so why even try? Shouldn't I just learn to live with them and ignore them?

I still find negative feelings inside of me, and I'm not proud of them, but they are a part of me. I've often wondered if I ought to express them in order to be my real self.

I have found the following verses of great assistance: "God's mighty weapons, not those made by men, [are used] to knock down the devil's strongholds. . . . With these weapons I can capture rebels and bring them back to God, and change them into men whose hearts' desire is obedience to Christ" (2 Cor. 10:3-5, LB).

As I discipline my mind and take hold of God's promises and power, my feelings are changed. I find I have a definite responsibility in this process. Many of my feelings are changed by awareness and acknowledgment, and then they actually become positive forces for good.

For example: When I admit to another, "Forgive me, I was wrong about that, you were right," my apology is usually accepted. Then I find I like that person better than I thought I would! In fact, I can understand how God can love that person because I find I can love her also.

DAY 9

Read Genesis 5:18–24.

Enoch walked with God.

Genesis 5:24, RSV.

"I get so discouraged trying to live a Christian life," my friend confided. "Some days are great, others not so good. Sometimes I am aware of God's presence and sometimes I am not. I want His presence all the time. Is this possible?"

Enoch walked with God day and night. He knew where God was (and of course God knew where he was). This fact alone gave him great confidence. Because the Holy Spirit is in our midst today, we too have knowledge of God's love and presence which brings us confidence.

It used to be that whenever I heard someone speak with quiet assurance about the reality of God's presence, I would become dissatisfied and hungry. I didn't have this reality, and I felt that God must love them more than He did me. I often said to Him, "How is it, Lord Jesus, that you give your presence to her and not to me? You said you were no respecter of persons." The answer came when I wanted to walk with God more than anything else in the world. Then I found the way to have His presence.

To walk with God cost Enoch something. It will cost us something, too. The test of my life is not what I am doing in times of great stress, but what I do in the humdrum existence of daily living. That in turn is the result of what I am, more than what I do.

To walk with God means being in union with Jesus Christ. This union comes to me through the life-giving power of His Spirit when I ask the new life of Jesus to be mine. I give up my own way of life, and begin to follow Jesus and His way of living. Walking and talking with God, I find that the more I look at Him, the less I look at myself. As John the Baptist put it: "He must increase, but I must decrease" (John 3:30, RSV).

DAY 10

Read 1 Peter 3:1–7.

The pious women of old who hoped in God . . . were submissive to their husbands—adapting themselves to them. . . .
1 Peter 3:5, Amplified.

A basic principle of marriage is that each partner must accept the other at face value; they must not try to change each other. That means that we must learn to fit in with our husband's plans, and learn to accept him as a person—just as he is.

Acceptance takes in many varied types of behavior: his personal habits, where he spends his extra time, his duties, social behavior, desires and dreams, accomplishments, money, relationship to children, religion, and so on.

You say, "Some of these need changing." Maybe they do, but if *you* try to do the changing, it will only cause more marriage problems than you already have. Love can be destroyed as real rebellion is aroused. In plain English, trying to change each other just does not work. If you are using this method—stop.

There is a solution, though it is not 100 percent sure. But giving other people freedom to be themselves will still allow them to grow and to be happy. God made us free moral agents, knowing that without freedom we are not able to mature. We can't change anyone, only God can.

A woman in my classes said to me, "I don't think I take away my husband's freedom when I insist that he improve. I never use force." C. S. Lewis says, "If we say we do not have a self-righteous attitude, we undoubtedly have one."

However, as women we unconsciously try to change our mates by nagging, pushing, criticizing, hinting—by disapproval, moral pressure, and suggestions. Check on yourself and notice how often you resort to one or more of these methods. It could surprise you.

Our attitude needs to be: "It's me, O Lord, standing in the need of prayer. I'm the one that must change. Start with me, Lord Jesus. I need to fit into my husband's plans."

DAY 11

Read Genesis 12:1–6.

[*I have heard the voice of the true God saying to me,*] *"Leave your land, your relatives and your father's household for a land I will show you, and I will make into you a great nation."*

Genesis 21:1, Berkeley.

When Abram told Sarai* what God had said to him and told him to do, her reply could easily have been, "A great nation? How can this be? We haven't an heir and I'm sixty-five years old. And, my husband, remember you are seventy-five. Are you *sure* God said this to you?" Abram could have answered, "I can't understand it, Sarai, but yes, I am sure God has spoken. I can't refuse to obey Him."

At sixty-five, Sarai must have been beautiful to look at. She had everything her heart could desire: servants to dress her and get her meals; a beautiful two-story house to live in surrounded by lush gardens. She had thick, rich, silky oriental rugs on her highly polished floors, hand-made linens, and pottery of finest craftsmanship. They lived in Ur of the Chaldees near the Persian Gulf.

Don't you suppose that Sarai was a bit upset when Abram told her they were to move? How do you react when you are happily situated, enjoying your home and community, and out of the blue your husband tells you that a move for him is imminent?

Let's see how Sarai reacted and what her attitude was. She watched while piece after piece of her precious handmade furniture and accessories were sold. She saved out a very few choice pieces to take with her, for their mode of travel was to be camel train. The entire

---

* Abram and Sarai were their names originally. Later they were changed to Abraham and Sarah, in line with God's promise to them about their son Isaac and their descendants. See Gen. 17.

pattern of their lives was being changed from that of city dwellers to the uncertain existence of semi-nomads of the desert. She could never hope for another house. She knew she would be living in a smelly, black goat-hair tent. That smell would never disappear, no matter how long the tents were used nor how cleverly she decorated them.

Sarai's reaction could have been, "Why does it have to be us, Lord? Why do we have to go so far? Can't we just move to another town so we don't have to be nomads?" She didn't say any of these things, she didn't complain, nor did she nag Abram. She respected him and loved him and submitted to his judgment. If he knew this was God's plan for them, then that was what she wanted. Even with this attitude, the cost to both of them was great.

It will cost you and me something to step out and follow God. Maybe you will be asked by Jesus to be the first one in your family to step out and commit your life to following Him. Maybe as a woman *you* will have to take the lead, following Abram's example. Many women who have done this have been rewarded as one by one the children and husband are brought into the "fold." It's an exciting experience, full of adventure, faith and daring.

DAY 12

Read Genesis 18:1–15.

Then God said to Abraham, "Why did Sarah laugh? Why did she say, 'Can an old woman like me have a baby?' Is anything too hard for God? Next year, just as I told you, I will certainly see to it that Sarah has a son."
Genesis 18:13, LB.

Three visitors appeared one day at Sarah's and Abraham's encampment. After the meal that Sarah prepared for them, the Lord (for the visitors were a manifestation of God) asked, "Where is Sarah?" It was customary for the woman not to appear at the table, but if she was like me, even though she was not included, she knew what was going on. Sarah didn't miss one thing that these men were saying for she was just behind the flap of the black goat-hair tent.

Then the Lord said to Abraham, "Next year I will give you and Sarah a son!" Sarah laughed silently as she thought, "A woman my age, have a baby?" And then she added, "And with a husband as old as mine?"

But God said to Abraham, "Why did Sarah laugh? Is anything too hard for God?" When Sarah heard this from her vantage point, she recognized that this was the Lord speaking. She had laughed only to herself and, besides, she was hidden from the men's view. She was afraid of this God who knew her very thoughts, how she felt, what she believed—every emotion in her—so she tried to excuse herself. "Well," she said, "I didn't laugh out loud." The Lord answered, "Oh yes, you did. I want to ask you, Sarah, is anything too hard for God?"

Read Hebrews 11:11–12 (LB) for the New Testament record of God's answer. Sarah's faith became active, and "she was able to become a mother in spite of her old age, for she realized that God, who gave her his promise, would certainly do what he said. And so a whole nation came from Abraham, who was too old to have even one child"!

DAY 13

Read Matthew 9:18–26.

If I may but touch his garment, I shall be whole.

Matthew 9:21, KJV.

The woman who said these words had been sick for twelve years. She had spent all her money in trying to get well, but "was nothing bettered, but rather grew worse" (Mark 5:26, KJV). As she heard about Jesus and all He was able to do, faith grew in her heart and she believed. "If I just touch His clothes, I'll be made well today."

With all the strength she had, she pressed through the crowd and touched Jesus. Jesus knew at once that power had gone out from Him, even though he was being jostled on all sides by the crowd (Mark 5:30–31). He stopped immediately and asked, "Who touched me?" When she admitted it, He said to her, "Daughter, thy faith hath made thee whole."

Jesus was surrounded by people who were sick, but worse than that, they were blind to His presence and power. All of them were witnessing miracles of healing, but she alone was healed, because she reached out and touched Him.

You have a pressing need today. Reach out and touch Him as this woman did. How can you do this? Get alone, open your Bible to this passage, get on your knees and talk to God about yourself. In your imagination, see yourself as the whole person He is going to make you, reach out your hand and while His presence is near and real, touch Him. In that instant He touches you also. This is faith. Then pour out the thanks and praise that is in your heart for the touch He has given to you.

Faith is what you believe about the person of Jesus Christ. Faith works by action. Faith works by praise. Touch Him and you, too, shall be made whole.

DAY 14

Read Matthew 10:1–8; Luke 6:30–38.

"Give as freely as you have received."
Matthew 10:8, LB.

"She is a charming person" is one of the things we like to hear about ourselves.

Charm is not only being soft-spoken, relaxed and at ease, it is being a good listener, it is responding, communicating, knowing how to give of ourselves to other people.

Charm is having a good memory for interesting and amusing things, so that we are happy and cheerful people. Others will seek us out, just to enjoy our company.

Charm adds a touch of magic to life. And the beauty of it is that it can be developed. Let's start with our tone of voice. Do we have have a cheerful soft-spoken voice? If not, Jesus said, "Ask, and you will receive, that your joy may be full" (John 16:24, RSV). Being cheerful on the telephone is part of giving. Yet, we often forget to ask God for a cheerful telephone voice. After we've asked for it, we need to run a check on ourselves and pray before we lift the receiver. Then see how the person on the other end responds. Try this magic on your husband. If it works on him, it will work on others.

God has given us many physical attractions to be used and shared. Any one of them can make our day worthwhile. Like taking extra care with our grooming, talking quietly, giving love, acting courteously, being liberal with praise for another, avoiding fault-finding. Any one of these will help us become charming persons.

DAY 15

Read 1 Peter 3:1–12.

Be beautiful inside, in your hearts, with . . . a gentle and quiet spirit. 1 Peter 3:4, LB.

A man once said to me, "You women have changed. You no longer permit a man to cherish you. I guess that is an old-fashioned idea, but on the other hand, you do allow us to support you."

Webster's dictionary says that the word *cherish* means "to adore, to hold dear, to feel or show special affection for; to keep and cultivate with care, to love and nurture." I decided then and there that if a woman is cherished it must be for both her inner and her outer beauty, and therefore beauty is worth working for.

The quality of inner beauty is voluntary. It is many things. It is laughter, cheerfulness, singing, smiling, being optimistic, having a sense of humor, bringing joy to others. It involves a quiet and gentle spirit as Peter suggests. Men find this fascinating in women—it is catchy, it calls for a response. The charm lies in the overall effect.

At their best, women's human qualities fascinate as well as amuse men. They want us to be totally feminine and to radiate happiness. They want us to have a fresh appearance and to be clean and neat. Sometimes we women underestimate these qualities and forget that they have great appeal. Women's magazines and cosmetic counters are filled with ways and means to look our best.

You can win your husband's love and be cherished if you will cultivate a gentle and patient spirit. But be feminine! Being bossy, cross or harsh does not contribute to feminine charm. No matter how hard you work for your husband, even doing what is usually considered his work, like mowing the lawn, painting the fence or the house—there always comes a time when you need to quit and to be feminine. This is because God made you to be a woman.

Peter says these characteristics are precious both to God and to your husband. Frankly, I work on being cherished.

DAY 16

Read Exodus 4:1–17

Moses pleaded, "O Lord, I'm just not a good speaker. I never have been, and I'm not now, even after you have spoken to me, for I have a speech impediment. . . . Lord, please! Send someone else."

Exodus 4:10, 13, LB.

Moses told God he did not want to be leader of the Israelites, even if they were God's chosen people. They wouldn't believe him. God answered Moses by giving him the power to do special signs and wonders.

But Moses was not satisfied with God's answer. He said, "I am not eloquent, . . . I am slow of speech."

God replied, "Who makes mouths? . . . Isn't it I, the Lord, who makes a man so that he can speak or not speak, see or not see, hear or not hear? Now go ahead and do as I tell you, for I will help you to speak well, and I will tell you what to say."

But Moses still wasn't persuaded. "Please send someone else," was his response.

Yet in spite of all his excuses, Moses didn't quit. Here are some of the factors that influenced him to change his mind, and obey God.

1. God revealed Himself to Moses as a living, loving God (Exod. 3:1–10).

2. Moses took time off, to be alone to pray and to meditate. He had no Bible, no books, no priests, only God to turn to. (Think that over.)

3. God said to Moses: "I am Jehovah, the Unchanging One" (Exod. 3:13–15). Imagine how awestruck Moses was to hear God give His name ("I am who I am," RSV).

4. God gave him a direct confirmation or sign of His presence when he was given the ability to perform miracles (Exod. 4:1–5).

5. When Moses still made excuses, even though he was fully equipped for work, God became angry and

rebuked Moses. He disciplined him for his excuses, but he also gave him a spokesman in his brother Aaron, so he wouldn't have to speak (Exod. 4:14–20).

Moses finally believed God. He responded by obeying God, expressing his faith by his actions. He faced up to his problems and returned to Egypt where men had tried to kill him. He had the power to return because he was a changed man, knowing that God was with him.

Today, people give the same excuses that Moses had. "I can't serve God because I'm not adequate. I'm fearful. I haven't enough education. I can't get up in front of people. I have a speech impediment. I can't use words well."

No one can have an experience with God and remain the same. When God calls you to serve Him, to speak for Him, He equips you and you are changed. And nothing is as powerful as *you*, when you move out for God.

DAY 17

Read Acts 7:17–36.

"Pharaoh's daughter found him [Moses] . . . and taught him all the wisdom of the Egyptians, and he became a mighty prince and orator."

Acts 7:21–22, LB.

Moses was given all the wisdom and learning of his day. Later he used it to write the first five books of the Bible. Pharaoh's daughter cared enough about him to take time to teach him herself. As a result he grew up to be mighty in word and deed. His early training showed throughout his entire life.

When Moses first tried to translate his faith into action, he was running ahead of God and he ended up killing an Egyptian. Then he suffered the humility of disgrace when his own king, the Pharaoh, tried to kill him. He had to leave Egypt and run away to the desert where he became a sheepherder and was forgotten by his people for forty years.

Moses had so many natural abilities and gifts that he found it easy to be self-sufficient. But at times he went to the other extreme and was unable to do anything right or to believe in himself, as we saw yesterday. I imagine his real handicap was a negative attitude toward God and toward life.

Can you identify with Moses and his problems? Do you find yourself going from one extreme to another? Are you alone in a desert? Is everything going wrong with you? Do you have a negative attitude toward life? toward God?

In his self-sufficiency Moses was trying to find himself. And in his own way, he was trying to fulfill God's plan for his life. What went wrong? He got in a hurry and moved out in his own strength without waiting for God and getting His plan. God had to humble him and give him the discipline he needed.

Like Moses, some of us have been taught well. We have been brought up correctly and have many talents and abilities, but we need discipline before God can use us. Maybe we need the discipline of staying at home and giving loving care to husband and children. Maybe we need to make them happy instead of trying so hard to make them good.

Moses finally turned over his whole life to God. God filled him and used him among his own people.

God is saying to us, "As I loved Moses, so will I love you. As I was with Moses so shall I be with you."

DAY 18

Read Mark 2:13-17.

I came not to call the righteous, but sinners to repentance.

Mark 2:17b, KJV.

As a committed Christian, I sometimes forget that I am "a sinner saved by grace." I find it hard to admit my humanity and to join those whom Jesus Christ loves, those whom He came to heal.

The great apostle Paul expressed his humanity in the 7th chapter of Romans—his inability to live up to what he knew was right and best. My attempt at expressing my humanity (sinfulness) runs something like this:

1. I want love and sympathy from my husband, but often, because of my disposition, I go about getting it the wrong way. This makes me really mad at myself and I feel guilty.

2. I work hard to impress certain people. Many times I can't understand why I do this, but I do it anyway, and then I feel guilty.

3. I find myself striving to be accepted as a teacher, when I should get all my approval from Jesus Christ, who is my teacher.

4. I find I do certain things and then say to myself, "Denise, a good Christian would not do or say what you just did. Are you a true believer or just a phony?" That adds more guilt.

5. I have real trouble understanding my own behavior sometimes, especially when I am happy and satisfied, and I give in to temptation; however, I immediately ask for forgiveness.

I take courage when I find that Paul did not understand himself (Rom. 7:15), and David (in the Old Testament) had the same problem. Like them, I confess my needs and failures and receive God's forgiveness. Each time I do, I remember that I am a member of the human race, and I need a Savior. Then I thank God for His forgiveness and His cleansing.

DAY 19

Read Mark 6:1–6, 53–56.

And as many as touched him were made whole.

Mark 6:56, KJV.

Have you touched Jesus recently? Touching Him is different from reading about Him, or praying to Him. Something always happens when we touch Him. Sometimes we can share our experience, and sometimes we can't, but we know a certain uplift, or quietness, or joy has come from Him to us.

How do we touch Jesus?
> Hope arises as we read about Him.
> Expectation is born and grows as we pray.
> Prayer brings "mental images" of the answer.
> Faith moves into action, and touches Him,
>> by our words, our thoughts, and even
>> by the hand of a friend who prays for us.

And then, having been made whole, there is
> Power to complete the job we feared,
> Patience to wait and to be quiet,
> Love to give the unlovable,
> Strength to say, I'm sorry;
> Fortitude to carry on,
> Peace in turmoil,
> Inward happiness in spite of outward harrassment,
> Praise and thanksgiving without visible evidence.

DAY 20

Read Mark 11:20–25.

Have faith in God. . . . What things soever ye desire, when ye pray, believe that ye receive them, and ye shall have them.
                        Mark 11:22, 24, KJV.

In these verses, Jesus is walking with His disciples and Peter calls His attention to the fig tree He had cursed which had now withered away. Jesus' answer to Peter was "Have faith in God."

There are several things we can say about this command.

First, "Have faith in God" means to have God's faith, the faith which God Himself has. That is, the Divine confidence in all that He says, in all that He does. God never wonders or doubts in His heart.

Second, this faith commands with authority. "Whosoever shall say unto this mountain, Be thou removed, and be thou cast into the sea; and shall not doubt in his heart, but shall believe that those things which he saith shall come to pass; he shall have whatsoever he saith."

Third, it is the faith which God gives to you. He does not suggest that you try to have it, but He gives it to you as a gift. When your faith fails, it's you, not He.

Fourth, if you are the possessor of this faith, you need not hesitate and doubt. You believe with joy and praise and thanksgiving.

The gift of faith is the God-given ability to believe God for the impossible. You are using God's faith to speak God's words in order that God's power may be released in you and through you. Meditate on this thought, repeat it until you know it, say it out loud, make it part of your life. This is your heritage.

With this faith, you can impart faith to others. God will direct you to speak words of faith which will produce faith, just as you can give courage and strength to others by the words you speak.

How to receive this gift:
1. Earnestly desire to receive—1 Cor. 12:31; 13:-13; 14:1.
2. Ask for it—John 16:24.
3. Follow instructions—Rom. 10:17.

DAY 21

Read Judges 6 and 7.

Gideon [said], "If the Lord is with us, why has all this happened to us?" . . . The Lord turned to him and said, "I will make you strong!" . . . But Gideon replied, "Sir, how can I save Israel? . . . I am the least thought of in the entire family!" Whereupon the Lord said to him, "But I, Jehovah, will be with you!"

Judges 6:13–16, LB.

Do you know this story about a little man who was fearful and afraid? "I'm a nobody," was his view. "What can I do? Why has this happened to me?" He reminds me of myself. I have said the same things.

Gideon was so afraid he would get out of God's will that he was anxious all the time. In his discouragement he talked to God about all the things that were happening to him and God answered him. The conversation could have gone something like this:

"Gideon, you are going into battle for me."

"That's fine, Lord, but I will not go unless you go with me."

"All right, I will go with you, but you will have to get rid of some of your soldiers."

"I will do just as you say, for the battle is Yours, not mine."

God kept reducing the number of soldiers until he had only 300 against 135,000 of the enemy. Israel won that battle because one man was willing to lead out of weakness when he knew God was with him. A miracle took place and all Gideon's fears were gone!

When you follow Gideon's example a miracle will take place in your life. Your fear will be gone and the battle will be won.

DAY 22

Read Ruth 1 and 2.

The Lord hath brought me home again empty.

Ruth 1:21, KJV.

Naomi spoke these desolate words out of the depth of feeling in her heart. She was honest about it when she said to the Lord, "Here I am coming home with nothing to show for the years I've slaved and sacrificed. I feel empty, despondent and alone."

When we think back over the past weeks of our life and do not see anything we have accomplished for God, we can identify with her. Such a feeling of emptiness! We pray, "Here I am again, Lord Jesus, empty handed. I have nothing to bring to you. I'm really inadequate, foolish, lazy and incompetent."

Naomi did not see how God had filled her hands. She did not see His planning for her life, nor did she know the joy of just giving herself to Him to be used by Him. She had not returned empty. Her daughter-in-law Ruth had come with her—Ruth, who became the grandmother of David, in the direct messianic line of our Lord.

Even though you are not aware of it, God has already put something or someone of value in your hands. You don't have to see it today or tomorrow. But look at the people God has put you with as His gifts. You are not empty or alone. Fill your heart and mind and mouth with praise and thanksgiving, for He cares for you.

DAY 23

Read Ruth 3 and 4.

"Just be patient until we hear what happens, for Boaz won't rest until he has followed through on this. He'll settle it today."
Ruth 3:18, LB.

Today's verse was spoken by Naomi to her daughter-in-law, Ruth, under the inspiration of the Holy Spirit. Ruth wanted Boaz to notice her as she was gleaning in his fields. Other men noticed her so why didn't he? When Ruth shared this with her mother-in-law, Naomi said something like this: "Be still, Ruth, don't be anxious, wait, pray and watch. God will tell you what to do. Just be ready and be His channel so He can work through you." God heard that prayer and brought Ruth to Boaz's attention. (God has such a gentle, kind, determined way of impressing on us what He wants from us.)

Ruth did not know she would marry Boaz, nor did she know she would be one of the five women in the genealogy of Jesus Christ to be mentioned by Matthew. She came to trust in God because her mother-in-law lived such a beautiful life. Ruth said, "She has something I do not have. I want to worship the God she worships." (Does your daughter-in-law want to serve Christ because you do?)

Ruth could have turned back at the halfway mark as they journeyed to Naomi's country (Ruth 1:14). To go on with her mother-in-law could have meant no relatives, no marriage, no family, no inheritance, no dowry—only poverty. Orpah, the other daughter-in-law, felt the price was too great and turned back to her old home.

Are you anxious and worried today over a personal problem? Take Naomi's advice to Ruth and don't worry and fret. Affirm in your mind these truths: *God is with me, working for me; this is His problem as well as mine. I will wait for His guidance. I will wait until I know "how the matter will fall"* (KJV).

DAY 24

Read 1 Samuel 3.

> *(Samuel had never had a message from Jehovah before.) . . . And the Lord came and called as before, "Samuel! Samuel!" And Samuel replied, "Yes, I'm listening."*
> 1 Samuel 3:7, 10, LB.

Have you discovered one of God's secrets—that He does not talk to you until you are ready to listen? Samuel did not know the Voice the first time it spoke to him. Eli the priest had to tell him who it was. When he knew it was God, he listened and answered.

What did Samuel do that we can do? Three things: he listened, he answered, he obeyed.

When Samuel listened he received a message from God to give to Eli. It was a judgment on the way Eli had raised his sons. These sons were undisciplined and had corrupted the worship of God. God held Eli responsible for the actions of his own children.

This message says to me that I am the person who must give discipline to my child in order to teach him what God is like. I learned many things about what God was like from my earthly father. By watching my mother I learned that love and devotion were to be given to God.

Nancy, the mother of two children, came to talk about the dissatisfaction in her life. She wanted her husband and her children to see the beauty of Jesus in her face. The two of us agreed and prayed together for this. When I saw her again at the end of six months, I marveled at the change in her. God had answered our prayers. Her entire family noticed the change in her. Her husband thanked me personally for praying for her.

In our world today, there are a few Samuels who hear God speak. But as Frank Laubach said, "God is speaking to all of us, all the time, all the time, all the time."

Listen . . . answer . . . obey.

DAY 25

Read Psalm 37:1–11.

Don't fret and worry—it only leads to harm.
Psalm 37:8, LB.

There seem to be so many important things I can't change, both in my life and in the lives of others I care about. Since I can't change them, why not just commit them all to God and leave them with Him. And so I do.

But it is not so easy with the smaller details: What shall I wear? What should I eat? What foods are not right for my condition? Did I unplug the coffee pot before I left this morning? Where did I leave my car keys? Oh, dear Lord, not again! Am I losing my mind or just getting old?

Worry is a nuisance! It robs me of a quiet and happy heart. I prefer to live without it, but it seems to be always with me. The best way to release it from my mind is to listen when God reminds me of the following words based on Philippians 4:4–7 (which I've memorized): *Denise, do not be worried about anything, but talk it over with Me and give thanks. Let Me know all your anxieties. . . . Then let My peace flow into your mind and your heart and there will be no room for worries of any kind, because I am in you and you are in Me.*

DAY 26

Read John 7:37–39 and the Scriptures in the text.

Now this he said about the Spirit, which those who believed in him were to receive; for as yet the Spirit had not been given, because Jesus was not yet glorified.

John 7:39, RSV.

Jesus tells us in this verse what He would give to anyone who believed in Him—the Holy Spirit. The gift would be given, He said, after He was glorified. His glory came after the crucifixion, after the resurrection, when He was taken up by the cloud and received by His Father.

Before he left them, Jesus instructed His disciples that He would return to His Father, but that He would not leave them alone or comfortless. He would return to them, in the person of the Holy Spirit (John 14:16–18).

It was in the upper room, on the Day of Pentecost, that the disciples were baptized in the Spirit. From that day, everyone who is united (converted) to Jesus Christ receives the gift of the Holy Spirit (Acts 11:15–17; 1 Cor. 12:13). Romans 8:9 further states that it is impossible to accept the Son and refuse the Holy Spirit.

There is, however, an experience of the Spirit, which some call "the baptism" and others call "the fullness" of the Spirit, which is available to all who hunger and thirst, to all who ask.

" 'Ask, and it will be given you; seek, and you will find; knock, and it will be opened to you. For every one who asks receives, and he who seeks finds, and to him who knocks it will be opened. . . . If you . . . know how to give good gifts to your children, how much more will the heavenly Father give the Holy Spirit to those who ask him?' " (Luke 11:9–13, RSV).

DAY 27

Read John 7:37–39; Acts 1:12–14; 2:1–14.

"Rivers of living water shall flow from the inmost being of anyone who believes in me." (He was speaking of the Holy Spirit. . . .)
John 7:38–39, LB.

The Holy Spirit is a gift to us from Jesus Christ and from His Father. Because you have accepted Jesus Christ as your Savior, you have a right to this gift.

One hundred twenty people were "filled with the Spirit" at Pentecost. Only twelve were apostles. Some were women who went home to cook, clean, sew, and wash for their families. Others were men who returned to their work in shops and fields. The promise of Jesus was fulfilled in that upper room. "Rivers of living water" flowed from them. It must have been an exciting, fulfilling and unforgettable event!

Being "filled with the Spirit" causes difficulty for many. Could it be because it involves simple acceptance of a free gift? We make it difficult because we insist on understanding, when being receptive is all that is needed to receive a gift.

My questions once were: How do I know I have the Holy Spirit? What difference will He make in my life? I'd like to share three things with you that have answered those questions.

First, I know I have the Holy Spirit because always there is a strong consciousness of the presence of Jesus living in me.

Second, I know, because He reproduces His life in me, which is the fruit of the Spirit. It's like apples being picked off the tree. The tree is not conscious of fruit being picked. Neither am I conscious of giving love, which Romans 5:5 says is the sign or mark of the Spirit. Friends often tell me they see the love of Jesus in me, and this never ceases to surprise me, although I admit it delights me at the same time.

Third, He gives me power to share my faith with others, and to be a witness for Him (Acts 1:8).

Finally, He gives me an intense desire to do His will, not mine. I know I am His child, and I know His Spirit lives within me.

DAY 28

Read Ephesians 5:15–20.

And do not get drunk with wine, for that is debauchery; but be filled with the Spirit.
Ephesians 5:18, RSV.

Are the filling of the Spirit and the baptism of the Spirit one and the same? We are not told this in black and white in the Scriptures, and everyone's experience is different. One baptism and many fillings is the way it reads in Paul's epistles. Be that as it may, Jesus told us that rivers of living water would pour through us when the Spirit came into us.

What are these rivers—that pour out, that fill us, that minister to us?

Romans 5:5 and 1 Corinthians 12 and 13 clearly state that love is the glowing badge of possession and ownership by the Holy Spirit. Love is the firstfruits of the Spirit, and all other fruits are included in it. Without love, I am nothing.

The branch which bears the fruit cannot see its own lovely clusters. The owner of the vineyard is delighted, as are all who see or eat the fruit.

Life abundant to share with all.

Love abundant to give to all.

These are the marks of one who is overflowing with God's Holy Spirit.

DAY 29

Read John 11:1–44.

> *Although Jesus was very fond of Martha, Mary, and Lazarus, he stayed where he was for the next two days and made no move to go to them.*
>
> John 11:5–6, LB.

Jesus was across the Jordan when he received word that his friend Lazarus was gravely ill. When He finally got to Bethany, the town where Martha, Mary and Lazarus lived, Lazarus was already dead. Why didn't Jesus go at once when he received news that Lazarus was seriously ill?

Because Jesus lived in the Father's will, whatever the Father's work was, that was His work. (Read John 5:19, 30.) His aim was not to do His own will, but the will of Him who sent Him. The delay meant not simply healing a sick man, but raising a dead man to life again.

Jesus was never in a hurry to get anywhere or do anything. He was never pushed by life or its circumstances, for He was in constant touch with His Father.

How can we avoid being in a hurry? Here is a woman who starts the day with the feeling, "I have so many things to do, I don't know if I'll ever get caught up." She is always a little behind, keeps everyone in her family waiting, and arrives at her destination out of breath. She is hurried from morning till night and carries her confusion with her everywhere she goes.

How can we avoid being hurried, so that we can be in the Father's will all day long, being a blessing wherever we go? The secret I have found is to spend a few quiet moments with my Lord before the day's work begins. I talk everything over with Him—my shopping list, telephone calls, the meetings I have to attend, the guests coming for dinner. I leave my husband and children in His protection. When I am through with my prayers, I have a list of things to do, and my heart is quiet.

DAY 30

Read John 15

I am the vine, ye are the branches: He that abideth in me, and I in him, the same bringeth forth much fruit: for without me ye can do nothing.

John 15:5, KJV.

There seems to be a false compulsion for activity that drives many Christians. One woman told me that she has to attend every special religious meeting she knows about. Another feels she must sell religious books in another city in order to be a good witness for God. Still another said, "There is something in me that drives me to be going and doing all the time. Why am I like this?"

What is the function of the branch? It is to stay joined to the vine and to bear fruit. What do I need to do when I am in union with Jesus (as the branch is in union with the vine)? The answer is: nothing. Absolutely nothing. All I need to do to accomplish His purpose is to remain on the vine and let His life pour through me.

The secret of the fruit is not in us—the branches—or in what we do or do not do. It is in the life that flows through us. This is a deceptive kind of passivity, for in union with Christ we stay where God has put us—on that vine—and our lives bear flower and fruit. In the fall we may drop our leaves and look bare and unattractive, but behold the spring comes and we are beautiful again.

Jesus teaches us in the 15th chapter of John that as we thus live in Him (and with Him) we find our fulfillment.

Hear His words: *I am the vine. You are the branches, drawing your strength, your wisdom, your peace, your comfort, your food, your power from Me. Without Me you can do nothing. I just want you to grow, mature, to bear flowers and have fruit. This takes place almost unconsciously as you go about your daily duties, in the home or in the office, knowing My life in you will be there, and that you are dependent on Me for everything.*

God never changes. But I change—I have my ups and downs. The important thing for me to remember is that it is the life of Jesus Christ within me that produces the fruit of the Spirit. (See Galatians 5:22–23.)

DAY 31

Read John 15

"You did not choose Me, but I chose you. And I planted you where you are in order that you should go and bear fruit."
John 15:16, KJ II.

When the revelation first dawned on me that God had chosen me before I chose Him, I became lost in the joy of this truth. To be chosen by Him, to know His love, to have His presence with me continually was almost more than I could take. In spite of the reality of this truth I was often puzzled because there were circumstances arising in my life which made me wonder if God still loved me. I had to learn that the unacceptable (to me) obstacles in my life did not change God's love for me.

I had to learn to "love my dandelions" like the retired gentleman I heard about. He had a fine lawn and kept it immaculate, except for the bright yellow dandelions which persisted in spite of all the expensive weedkillers he tried. He wrote a garden expert about his difficulty and received this reply. "If none of the suggestions I have enclosed work, I suggest you learn to love dandelions."

Most of us have dandelions we have to learn to love, in the form of a person who needs to be appreciated or a circumstance that needs to be accepted.

Jesus is saying today: I have placed you in the circumstances you are in because I love you. Your work, your home, your husband, your children—I have given them to you as part of My plan for you. It is not by chance that you attend that certain church, or that you have those specific neighbors. Right where you are living is where you can bear the best fruit for Me.

My reply: Lord Jesus, because you chose me and planted me in my home in Seattle, Washington, I will love "my dandelions." I can bear fruit right where I am. Thank you for choosing me before I chose you.

Bloom where you are planted!

Second Month

DAY 1

Read Zephaniah 3:14–20.

For the Lord your God has arrived to live among you.
He is a mighty Savior.
He will give you victory.
He will rejoice over you in great gladness;
He will love you and not accuse you.
  Zephaniah 3:17–19, LB.

Is this a joyous choir I hear?

No, it is the Lord Himself rejoicing over me in happy song. Amazing thought. The Lord singing a song about me? The Lord rejoicing over me? The Lord loving me? He knows my name? I bring joy to Him?

What a humbling, delightful experience! I read the words over and over until I know them by heart. My mind and my spirit will be refreshed and revived each time I remember or repeat these joyous words.

DAY 2

Read Psalm 91.

For he shall give his angels charge over thee, to keep thee in all thy ways.
Psalm 91:11, KJV.

Remember when you were a child in Sunday school and you were told that an angel went with you all the time to protect you and to watch over you? I was told by one teacher that the angel was always there on my shoulder, even if I couldn't see him, because Jesus had assigned him to take care of me. I remember how much comfort and security that gave me, how nice and warm it made me feel.

God is the same, yesterday, today and forever. He watches over you continually, all through your life. Believe this and trust Him completely, for He will never let you down or disappoint you.

Another thing—remember that He keeps you in all of your ways, not just in part of them, not just sometimes, but all the time!

Become childlike in your trust and look to Jesus for guidance. He will bring peace and security to your mind. You need never be lonely, nor afraid, for His angel is with you. (The angel is really God's Holy Spirit with you and in you.)

The secret is simply to put yourself in God's hands, and let Him take charge of you.

DAY 3

Read 1 Samuel 25:18–35.

"The soul of my lord shall be bound in the bundle of life with the Lord thy God."
1 Samuel 25:29, KJV.

"I cannot possibly believe God loves me," a woman wrote to me, "and that He cares about all the little problems in my life. Of course, I believe He loves the world and all His marvelous creation—but us little humans—no, I just can't believe that."

In the verse written out at the top of this page, God is telling David (through Abigail) something each one of us would like to hear for ourselves: how much God loves us and cares for us.

In effect, God was saying to David, "You are a very special person to Me. I am in you and you are in Me. We are united, we are one, we are bound up together in this life. What you experience and suffer, I experience and suffer. When you rejoice and have great joy, so do I. I chose you. I need you, even as you need Me. I am your close Friend and Counselor."

Can you imagine the effect this assurance had on David? Yet Jesus, through the words in the New Testament (John, chapters 14 and 15), is saying these things to you today.

In the final analysis, we all live our lives alone, and our greatest help comes from God and His Word. Yet in His wisdom, our Father knows we need a human friend to love us, to strengthen and encourage us, as Abigail strengthened David.

Do you have a friend in whom you can confide, with whom you can pray and share the joy which comes when God answers your prayers? If you don't, ask Him for one. (Read Matt. 7:7, 8.)

Because you are wrapped in the bundle of life and love with your Lord, take courage. God loves and cares for you.

DAY 4

Read 1 Samuel 24; 30:1–8; Psalm 54.

> *But David encouraged and strengthened himself in the Lord his God.*
> *1 Samuel 30:6,* Amplified.

Why did David need to encourage and strengthen himself?

Because his family and the families of his men had been taken prisoner. But more than that, King Saul had deliberately showed hatred toward David and had tried to kill him. What was David's reaction? He showed love and concern every time. "I did not take advantage of you, because I care about you. You are God's chosen servant and I will not lift my hand against you" was his attitude.

What did this do to Saul? The Bible says the house of Saul grew weaker and weaker while the house of David grew stronger and stronger. You may say that what happened to David was unjust. True, but that is not the point. The point is, it was his attitude in the midst of this animosity that strengthened him.

Saul was David's cross, and because David's attitude was right, the cross became his crown.

Your cross could be your mother-in-law, brother-in-law, husband, child, neighbor, minister, or church. When someone is nasty and mean to you because you love Jesus, that is what we call a cross. When this happens, you can identify with David and know how he felt.

How did David strengthen and encourage himself?

David wrote down his experiences, his successes, his failures, his joys, and his sorrows; then he talked to God about them. You can read all about them in the Psalms. He did more—he listened to what God had to say to him, and then he did what he was supposed to do.

The Book of Psalms is a beautiful book which will strengthen and encourage you if you will take time to get into it, and stay in it. Listen to what God is saying to you and do what he tells you.

Life's difficulties are not intended to arrest your progress but to help you grow and live an abundant life in the Spirit. Every step of your way is planned. As a believer, all you have to do is acknowledge the Presence of Jesus near you, for He is there. Keep the channels of love and forgiveness open so He can work in you and through you.

Help yourself to the treasures David has left for you, that you may be strengthened, encouraged and comforted.

DAY 5

Read 1 Kings 3:1–15.

"O Lord my God, now you have made me the king instead of my father David, but I am as a little child who doesn't know his way around. . . . Give me an understanding mind."
1 Kings 3:7, 9, LB.

King David was dead and his son Solomon had been crowned king. Solomon had leaned heavily on his father. He watched him work mighty acts through faith and prayer. He saw how God used his father to bless people. He saw reality and honesty in David's life. God was as real to David as we are to each other. Solomon even saw "the glory of God" come upon his father, and heard him give the glory back to God in everything that happened. He took none of the glory for himself.

But now David was dead, and Solomon as the new king was left alone with the kingdom. He found that the hardest thing for him to do was to keep a balance between doing God's will and his own will. He was naturally a proud man and loved approval and pleasure, position and popularity, pomp and power. Besides all this, he had about a thousand wives and concubines. Yet in spite of all these things which continually pulled him in the opposite direction, he had a heart to do God's will.

It was not wrong for Solomon to depend upon David when he was alive. But there always comes a time when the one we depended upon has to move on. How does one accept this? How does one strike a balance in such a dilemma? The present circumstances and the uncertain future threaten to pull us away from God's will. The answer—simply tell God all about it: "I can't go on alone. I can't make it by myself."

Solomon admitted that he couldn't go on without his father who knew how to handle people. "I am as a little child who doesn't know his way around. . . . Give me an understanding mind."

God answered Solomon by giving him the wisdom he needed. And He promised to be with Solomon (1 Kings 9:3).

You must remember that God is with you, that He is planning for you. God is saying to you, "I will never leave you. You will not be alone for I will always be with you. I am the same yesterday, today and forever."

With this promise, you have to pick up the pieces and go ahead—and you can do it, for He is with you.

DAY 6

Read 1 Kings 10:1–13.

Blessed is the Lord your God, who delighted in you to set you on the throne.
1 Kings 10:9, KJ II.

These words of tribute were spoken by the Queen of Sheba to Solomon. She had traveled 1250 miles from her kingdom in Arabia (today the territory of Yemen) where she reigned over the Sabeans, and she had come for the express purpose of verifying the reports of the splendor of Solomon's kingdom, the temple of the Lord, and his great wisdom.

We are never told whether she actually became a believer in Solomon's God, but her words are significant in showing us her respect and acceptance of all she heard and saw.

No doubt she was impressed by the happiness and contentment she saw reflected in the faces of Solomon's people, as much as she was with the great riches and affluence spread out to receive her.

She might have said, "Being accustomed to pomp and plenty, art and luxury, as a Queen I thought I had seen everything, but now I find I have seen nothing. The half was not even told to me: there is no spirit left in me. I am overwhelmed, and I give you my blessing."

The Queen of Sheba did not believe until she saw for herself. Many of us are like her. We have heard about the new life of the Spirit, we have listened to hearsay, we have heard second-hand accounts of miracles in the lives of those who wholly give themselves to Jesus Christ, but we have never made the decision to see for ourselves.

Here are a few guidelines on how to find out for yourself about the new life in Christ: Go to the right place for help. Bring your questions into the open. Come in the right spirit to receive—not critical, but receptive. Bring tokens and gifts to show your appreciation.

The half has never yet been told!

DAY 7

Read 1 Kings 17.

> *This is a beautiful story of a man led by God to the home of a widow, where he became a blessing to her, and she in turn, to her community. As you read this chapter, ask God to help you apply some of these thoughts to your own life.*

Elijah was a very important man, yet he had to endure discipline or "conditioning" from God in order to be used of God. He was disciplined in courage, in loneliness and in love.

God has to discipline us before we are ready for His service. His purpose for us is not dependent on our age, our education or lack of it, or our circumstances. He wants to use us to bless our generation.

What is the secret of discipline? Prayer. Look at Elijah again. He knew God changed people and circumstances through prayer, so he prayed and let God change *him* first.

How can we accept this discipline? We need to try putting ourselves in Elijah's place and saying to God, "I'll prove you. I want changes to be made in my life, in my family, in my circumstances. I know this means starting with me, but I'm willing, Lord."

Look again at Elijah's circumstances. Whether or not your situation is as difficult as his, God is still sovereign. He is the same yesterday, today, and forever. Prayer is still the answer.

You might say, "My husband left me. My mother-in-law doesn't understand me. I have an incurable disease. My son is on dope. My children only care about themselves. I can't get along with my neighbors."

Prayer is still your answer. Talk to God about yourself, about every detail of your life. If you will voluntarily choose to let him "condition" your life with prayer, He can make you a great blessing to your family, to your neighbors—just as He made Elijah a blessing to others.

Elijah prayed and God answered.

You pray and God will answer.

DAY 8

Read 1 Kings 18:1–19:7.

And as [Elijah] lay and slept under a juniper tree, behold, then an angel touched him, and said unto him, Arise and eat.
1 Kings 19:5, KJV.

Elijah had just finished demonstrating to the people of Israel on a grand scale that the Lord was the one true God. His dramatic confrontation with the prophets of Baal had ended with their complete destruction.

But when Queen Jezebel had heard the news that her prophets had been killed, she reacted in fury toward Elijah, cursing him, and vowing to kill him. From the exaltation of Mt. Carmel, Elijah had to turn tail and flee into the wilderness. There great depression followed the exaltation and fear that had driven him. Self-pity and despair came next, as he wished for death to overtake him at once.

As he lay under a juniper tree, he asked God to take his life, for nothing had meaning any more. Exhausted from his journey and his fears, he fell asleep. It was the best thing he could have done.

Sometimes when we are under great stress we should follow Elijah's example—tell God just how we feel, then go to bed and sleep it off. When we awaken, we are refreshed and things never look as tragic as they did the night before.

Elijah knew God had heard him, because an angel awakened him and told him, "Arise and eat." Here is another ordinary remedy to add to sleep. Both food and sleep restore us in times of sorrow or fear. Elijah got up, ate, and waited for the next thing the Lord had for him.

When God awakens us from our rest, He always has something special for us to do. Let us remember that the next time depression hits. God is still there, still with us, ready to use us.

DAY 9

Read 1 Kings 19:7–18.

The children of Israel have forsaken thy covenant . . . and I, even I only, am left; and they seek my life, to take it away.
1 Kings 19:14, KJV.

After Elijah had eaten what the angel had provided for him in the wilderness, he was told to travel to Mt. Horeb in the Sinai peninsula. There he stayed in a cave to see what else the Lord would say.

When the Lord spoke to Elijah he said, "What are you doing here? Why are you hiding in that cave?" Elijah answered right out of his heart, not hiding the way he felt about what was happening. He informed God how hard he had worked and how wicked the world was. He thought everything depended on him, he was the only righteous man left, and they were trying to kill him. "I, only I, am left." *Poor old me, why do I have to go on alone?*

Elijah had a do-it-yourself temperament, but right now he was on an emotional see-saw. He had tried to play God—to show how well everything turned out when he ran it. *My, I'm proud of what I've been doing to help you, Lord. See what I have contributed to your cause!* But when things didn't work well, he was discouraged and full of self-pity. *I'm a failure! What is the use? Why try?*

The do-it-yourself wife can't trust her husband. She checks on him constantly until it annoys him. She can't trust him to be the head of the family. She doesn't admire his strengths and his good points. She interferes with all his decisions and makes him lose face. She is selfish, putting herself and her wishes before his. She takes on all the family burdens.

The do-it-yourself husband doesn't trust his wife in anything. He questions the money she spends, he doubts her wisdom, her discipline of the children, her decisions. He robs her of peace of mind, and tries to shoulder all the family responsibilities.

The do-it-yourself boss never trusts his employees to follow directions. He constantly hovers over them, checking on their work, robbing them of initiative, making them feel incapable. And the do-it-yourself employee goes ahead without checking with his boss, taking matters into his own hands that don't belong there.

The do-it-yourself person, like Elijah, is often harried, hurried, burdened with the responsibilities of life. He simply has not learned to cultivate a childlike spirit, which gives God control, and which trusts other people. Periodically, he retreats into his cave of self-pity.

There is no complete solution to the human traits of self-sufficiency and self-pity. But the cave is a copout. There is a safe balance to be found in listening to God, as Elijah did. For God can break into our self-pity.

Elijah was told to go out and stand on the mountaintop. There he first experienced a great wind, then an earthquake, then a fire. But the Lord was not in any of them. Just as he was wondering if he had made a mistake and misunderstood God's instructions, he heard that still small voice. This was the Lord God! All the fear, the loneliness, the discouragement, the self-pity left him as he experienced the presence of God, and listened to God's words.

"Others struggle with these problems and find their way to Me through them," is God's word to us as to Elijah. "My work in this world is still going on. Get in there and work with Me. Forget yourself and get busy helping someone less fortunate than you."

There is the answer to self-pity.

DAY 10

Read Psalm 46.

> God is our refuge and strength, a very present help in trouble.
>
> Psalm 46:1, KJV.

Substitute the personal pronoun *my* or *me* instead of *our* in this verse. "God is *my* refuge and *my* strength, a very present help in trouble for *me*." Now it becomes a personal message for you. When a particular trouble looms ahead, before you do anything else, repeat this verse six or eight times. Then pray for yourself and your troubles within the framework of this verse.

What you need from God is comfort, protection, and healing. You want strength to stand up to the trouble and meet it head-on. Remind yourself that God is with you, that He loves you, that He will never leave you or forsake you. Say these words, "God is with me, helping me, right now. He is my refuge. He is my strength."

These are very simple suggestions but they will give you a sense of comfort and joy. New hope will flood your mind. New ideas will come to you so that you can help yourself. A new sense of power will well up within you. The result: you will be able to rise above the entire situation.

DAY 11

Read Romans 8:26–39.

And we know that all things work together for good to them that love God, to them who are the called according to his purpose.
Romans 8:28, KJV.

My husband and I were on vacation in Maui, Hawaii, when he became ill with a bleeding ulcer. I called a doctor friend in Honolulu, who assured me that he would have an ambulance at the airport to meet us. We arrived near midnight, and Lloyd was put in the ambulance which took off for the hospital. I was left with all the luggage.

Six different cab drivers refused to take me where I wanted to go. "We only go to Waikiki. We can't take you." Finally I was the only passenger left in the interisland airport. The porter said to me, "Madam, you will have to stand outside, as I am closing the doors until morning." I had never felt so alone and forgotten.

Suddenly I remembered Romans 8:28: "All things work together for good." What was God trying to teach me in this situation? Wearily I leaned back and shut my eyes. It looked like disaster because not only would I miss my next connection, but the friends waiting for me would be worried. I started to talk to God, but before I had finished my prayer, a taxi stopped in front of me. "Lady," the driver said, "I just couldn't forget you; I was so frustrated I had to turn around and come back for you."

As I thought about this experience later, a number of thoughts came to me. A general faith in God is good, but when a specific situation arises, one needs to have faith at that very time. A specific faith for a specific thing. When I prayed specifically, I found I could handle my situation. I could respond quietly to the taxi driver and later to my friends instead of being all shook-up. In that quick moment of prayer, when the answer was already on the way, God took from me all the self-pity and frustration and gave me His peace.

This could have been a major crisis in my life, but because I trusted the Lord and knew He loved me, everything worked out for good.

DAY 12

Read Romans 10:1–21.

Faith cometh by hearing, and hearing by the word of God.

Romans 10:17, KJV.

Sometimes women at conferences ask me how I get so much from the Bible incident from which I am teaching. To answer them, I often give a brief description of my method of study.

First, there is the careful detailed study of the text itself, taking in the persons, the place, the actions, and the ideas. Then there is the arranging of lessons learned so that those listening can apply God's truth to their own lives.

Let's take Mark 5:25–34 as an example.

Persons: Who is mentioned here? Write their names down.

Place: On a street (?).

Actions: Using the verbs, make a simple outline of what happened.

These three things are all based on black and white words in the text—facts, in other words. Now we are ready for the fourth ingredient, which is *ideas.*

Here you are free to use your imagination, and to identify with the little woman who was ill for twelve years. As you follow the action in your imagination, then describe it, your own voice speaking of the power of Jesus will fill your heart with expectation of what He can do for you.

We might say that the fifth ingredient is application. How can this be applied to you, your situation, your need?

Try selecting a story from the Gospels and working out the details and application yourself. Then share the lesson learned with someone, for it is by hearing that faith is born.

DAY 13

Read 1 Corinthians 11:1–3.

But I want you to know that Christ is the head of every man, the head of woman is her husband, and the Head of Christ is God.
1 Corinthians 11:3, KJ II.

Here is a true story on how this verse became a reality in one woman's life.

"After attending one of your classes, I went home determined to be a better wife and mother. I was doing fine until we went on a vacation. Then I fell into my old habit of telling my husband what to do. There were decisions to be made daily, and I made them! I kept offering suggestions, which slyly inferred that my way is the best way after all. It wasn't long until I noticed that cool far-away attitude in my husband's eyes.

"I remembered what we learned in your classes, about pressuring people, and about letting my husband be head of our family. I asked God for wisdom and He gave it to me.

"The following week I resolved not to offer one suggestion unless I was asked. He didn't ask once! Believe me, it wasn't easy but I did it. I put an X on paper every time I was tempted to give advice or act superior in any way. The paper was covered with Xs.

"I learned four things on that vacation.
1. I shouldn't act like I know more than my husband does.
2. I shouldn't be motherly; I am a wife.
3. I shouldn't talk man-to-man language. He wants me to be a woman.
4. I should always make him feel superior in his role as head of our household.

"By the end of our vacation we were back to loving each other and life was beautiful. I said a heartfelt 'Thank you, Lord,' for giving me a husband who can take care of me."

DAY 14

Read 2 Corinthians 4:7–18.

I believe and therefore I speak.
2 Corinthians 4:13, LB.

Four young married women were meeting for coffee one morning each week while their children were in pre-school. One day one of them shared an answer to her prayers. She was so excited about it that the whole group was affected. Soon the coffee-klatch became a spiritual gathering instead of a social one. They all wanted to experience what their friend had experienced. (Sometimes we think that what happens to us is not important, but that is not true. Enthusiasm is highly contagious, and makes others want what we have.)

These women decided to pray for each other. Every week they brought their requests for their husbands, children, friends and neighbors. They decided not to tell anyone, not even their husbands, about these little prayer sessions until they were positive their prayers were being answered.

After about three weeks, things started to happen. Husbands began asking questions: What's going on? What changed you? Why are you so concerned about my welfare? How come you are so kind? You haven't kept me waiting lately, how come? You aren't nagging or complaining, what's going on?

Then the truth came out: "We are praying about our problems, about ourselves and our responsibilities. We check up on each other, to see that our love is real, not superficial. We can talk honestly with each other without being critical. We are learning what it means to put God first. The Bible has come alive as we study together.

"Our times of praise and thanksgiving were slow at first, but now they are the highlight of our week. As we learn to share with each other, we are able to share with our neighbors. We are at ease and comfortable with each other; there is no pressure, only joy and fulfillment."

This group of women grew to eight, then to sixteen, and their entire church was affected. As a result, small groups were formed throughout their congregation and many, many lives are being changed.

The effectual prayers of righteous women avail much (James 5:16).

DAY 15

Read 2 Corinthians 10:1–6.

Casting down imaginations, and every high thing that exalteth itself against the knowledge of God, and bringing into captivity every thought to the obedience of Christ.
2 Corinthians 10:5, KJV.

The greatest battle the Christian has is the battle of the mind. For instance: You pass another woman and she does not recognize you. Immediately your mind starts to work—that woman doesn't like me; she never even noticed me; I believe she did that on purpose; she has never liked me; she despises me, so I despise her.

The next day you get the flu and have to stay in for a few days. Your pastor neglects to visit or call you, so now you are thinking of not voting for him for recall. Well, you never really did like him too well, anyhow.

Both these situations are strongholds for Satan to work on. If the woman who seemed to be slighted had immediately given her thoughts to God, they would never have grown to such proportions. We need to use His Name in prayer as a powerful weapon to cast out these negative imaginations. And we need to do it at the very moment they arise in our minds.

The words of 2 Corinthians 10:5 can help you harness God's power in your moment of need. If you choose to discipline your thoughts and move out toward God, you can be the most powerful tool God has to cast out Satan.

Use these three points to bring your thoughts into captivity for Christ as often as necessary.

1. Recognize the source when you are negative.
2. Call it by its right name.
3. Accept Christ's forgiveness and praise Him.

DAY 16

Read 2 Corinthians 10:7–18.

Do you look on things after the outward appearance?

2 Corinthians 10:7, KJ II.

Paul is talking to us here about the way we measure one another. Here are some of the things I personally struggle with: I look at a woman's outward appearance. What is she wearing? I find myself trying to measure whether she is a good Christian or not by the way she looks and dresses. Whether she is fulfilling her personality. Whether she is making any kind of success of her marriage. Because these things are important to us, we get hung-up on them.

In 2 Corinthians 10:7–13 Paul gives us two measures to help us make judgments. First, he writes that the false apostles (cunning and persuasive) measure their Christian status by each other and by their neighbors—what they did and what they said. They measured themselves by themselves and in this showed that they lacked wisdom (v. 12).

Second, Paul included himself. "I measured myself by God's standards, what He wants from me and for me." He points out that these false apostles will always be with us. We have to decide which is which. Some people decide by outward appearance but God looks at the heart. We have to watch carefully here or we'll get into trouble.

A friend of mine who was praying about her husband told me that God spoke to her and told her to do a certain thing, assuring her He would take care of the outcome. When I heard her story, I said, "I believe you will be in deep trouble if you go ahead. What you have told me is against what God is saying in the Bible in regard to husbands and wives." We sat down together, checked it out in our Bibles, prayed together, and she saw it for herself.

God is at the same time both our judge and our

lover, for He looks at the heart. We *must* search our Bibles for truth. We must ask God for His kind of love for one another. We must often remind ourselves of Anna Mow's astute comment, "Man cannot sit on the judge's seat and the lover's seat at the same time."

DAY 17

Read 1 Peter 2:18–3:6.

Wives, fit in with your husbands' plans; for then if they refuse to listen when you talk to them about the Lord, they will be won by your respectful, pure behavior. Your godly lives will speak to them better than any words.

1 Peter 3:1–2, LB.

A lady living in the Hawaiian Islands told Ros this story:

I had hurried through my dinner dishes, grabbed my Bible, and was going out the door as I called to my husband, "Goodbye, I'm on my way to church."

"Don't hurry," he called after me. "I really don't care whether you come back or not. Why don't you move your bed down there too?"

His response floored me. I couldn't believe my ears! What had happened to our marriage?

It didn't take me long to spot the trouble. I was spending almost every evening of the week in some kind of church work, yet I wasn't conscious that my husband's resentment was building up. But when he made that comment, I knew things had to change. But how?

Well, I learned and learned fast that I was reversing God's order and that was what was primarily wrong. I felt I didn't have enough hours to spend time with four children, a husband, *and* church work, so I put my husband last. That was my big mistake. As soon as I realized that, I reversed this order, and began to put my husband first.

I had completely overlooked the fact that God made me to be a wife first, a mother second, and then a homemaker. To give my husband the appreciation he needed, I began to make up for lost time. I started to admire him, to build up his ego, to thank him for providing for me.

Then I asked God to give me back my real love and

joy in being with him. That was answered. I found love draws out love. In the response of giving and receiving love, we both found new fulfillment.

I accepted him as he was and placed myself under his protection. I gave him his rightful place as head of the family. I verbally and actually gave love, and our home became a happy place. It took a near tragedy to wake me up, but I thank God for moving me to action.

DAY 18

Read 2 Kings 2:1–15.

> *"He took the mantle of Elijah and struck the waters and said, Where is the Lord God of Elijah? And when he hit the waters, they parted and Elisha went over."*
>
> 2 Kings 2:14, KJ II.

LUCY: "You know what the whole trouble with you is, Charlie Brown?"

CHARLIE BROWN: "No, and I don't want to know, just leave me alone."

LUCY: "The whole trouble with you is, you won't listen to what the whole trouble with you is."

Elisha was in trouble and knew where the whole trouble was—himself. He had been listening to Elijah, who warned him about the future, and who had given him examples of what was expected of him. Finally, Elijah was gone, and Elisha had to face up to his problem alone.

The school of young prophets was watching him, so Elisha felt he had to do something and do it right away. He had to move out and overcome his fears: the fear of God not answering his prayers, the fear of people seeing him fail, the fear and discouragement of being alone. He faced frustration, hostility and weakness.

Finally he said to himself, "Where is the God of Elijah?" In other words, "If God is for me, who can be against me," and with that promise on his lips, he struck the waters with Elijah's mantle, and behold! the waters parted, and he crossed over to the other side! God was with him! God did answer him!

Elisha faced his problem and his fears with God's help. He turned first to God for help, not to a human friend. Then, he used what God had made available to him—Elijah's mantle—for his solution. The result was that God showed His power and His glory to the young prophets through Elisha, and they accepted him as their new leader.

Some of us are just like Elisha. We say, "Where is God? I can't do this work by myself. I haven't the ability. Let Mrs. Jones do it—she has more gifts than I do."

We need to stand on the same truth Elisha stood on. If God is for me, who can be against me (Rom. 8:31)? Repeat it. Memorize it. Believe it! Use it!

"I sought the Lord, and he answered me, and delivered me from all my fears. O taste and see that the Lord is good! Happy is the man who takes refuge in him!" (Ps. 34:4, 8, RSV).

DAY 19

Read 2 Kings 4:1–7.

"What shall I do for you? Tell me; what have you in the house?"

2 Kings 4:2, RSV.

Elisha asked this question of the widow whose husband, a seminary student, had died and left her with debts. Her creditors were threatening to take her two sons into slavery if she didn't pay them.

Elisha could have said, "If you'll follow my directions, I can help you." But he didn't, he just went step by step and the miracle took place.

"What do you expect me to do about your debts?" Elisha asked. "Let's see what you have in your house."

"I have nothing, sir, but a jar of olive oil."

Elisha told her to go to the neighbors and borrow all the jars she could find. The woman did exactly as she was directed. Elisha blessed that little jar of olive oil, and told her to pour oil into the borrowed jars until they were all full. Then he told her to go and sell the oil, pay her debts and live on the rest.

There was no fuss or confusion about this miracle. There was a specific request and a definite answer. And the answer came through something she already had in her possession.

In your life, there is something you can use, something God can bless to meet your needs. And if you look around, you may also find a man or woman of God who will pray for you and give you God's blessing.

"Ask, and you will receive, that your joy may be full" (John 16:24, RSV).

DAY 20

Read 2 Kings 4:8–37.

Gehazi passed on before them and laid the staff on the face of the child. But there was no voice or hearing, and he went back to meet [Elisha] and told him, The child has not awakened.

2 Kings 4:31, KJ II.

Reading about Gehazi, we can quickly see what his trouble is. He knows too much, talks too much, and gives advice without being asked. He probably felt he was a self-made authority because he was Elisha's servant and knew all the doctrines. Yet the end of the story shows that his life had no fruit of power, or joy, or peace.

You probably know people like Gehazi. They are good fundamental Christians, but their religion seems to be more in their minds than their hearts. They know all the right answers, and they believe every word in the Bible.

Perhaps the question should be, are you like Gehazi? Someone comes to you for help and you have no power, no witness, no answered prayer, no miracles to share with them. You know all the steps and verses, but you can't bring anyone to know Christ personally.

Look again at Gehazi. He did exactly what he had seen Elisha do to that child, but he did not hear any voice, nor did God speak. He had to return to Elisha and admit defeat. Admission of defeat because of self-effort is one of the first places to start.

Some years ago I was praying that God would change some things in our home that I couldn't change. God started with me, telling me to set my loved ones free instead of pressuring them to do what I wanted. Another "word" from Him came through loud and clear regarding my husband: "You make him happy, and I'll make him good."

We need power to minister to our loved ones, to submit to and respect our husbands, and to train our children. Often there is "no voice or hearing" because we have asked for nothing. We need to be good administrators in our homes, keeping things in order, not being extravagant. We need God's help in making our homes happy peaceful places for our families to live in.

What was Elisha's power? As we read about his life and the miracles he performed, we find an attitude of complete surrender to God. He chose to meet each day trusting in the power of the Lord his God. This is the attitude we must have. Each day we must have something direct from God in order to have something to give away to another.

Lord, I want Your way, not mine.
I surrender myself completely to You.
I choose to meet this day in the power of Your Holy Spirit.

DAY 21

Read 2 Chronicles 20:1–30.

> *He appointed singers unto the Lord, and that should praise the beauty of holiness.*
> 2 Chronicles 20:21, KJV.

When we read that Jehoshophat appointed singers and praisers to go before the army and sing praises, we must remind ourselves that this was before they engaged in battle, and the enemy was as yet unseen. They were praising God for a victory which was assured to them by faith, but which they had not yet experienced. So sure were they of the coming victory, that all the people began to praise God as they marched along. And at that very moment the Lord confused the enemy so that they began to fight among themselves!

There was one day that my conversation with God went something like this:

"I know terrific powers are set up against me for today."

My Father replied: Why are you behaving as a small child? You must remember, "Greater is he that is in you, than he that is in the world" (1 John 4:4, KJV).

So I began to praise God. I praised Him that His Spirit within me was able to cope, even if I could not. I praised Him for every detail of my situation.

Then quietness began to steal over my spirit and into my body, and I found myself watching Him release His power to work in my behalf.

Praise is for today, for now. Praise is believing that God's perfect will is being worked out, that I can trust and sing now. Praise is total and joyful acceptance of the *now*.

This means that God wants us to march on with a song of praise in our heart. He wants us to be one of His singers. To stand with our believing friend or friends, and sing together when we know there is a battle ahead.

DAY 22

Read Ephesians 1.

> How we praise God, the Father of our Lord Jesus Christ, who has blessed us with every blessing in heaven because we belong to Christ.
>
> *Ephesians 1:3,* LB.

When I used to read this verse in the King James Version, I always wondered what it meant when it said we had been blessed with all "spiritual blessings." It was a wonderful day when I made the discovery that these spiritual or heavenly blessings are for earthly use. Here are some of them: forgiveness, maturing, prayer, praise, worship, the church, other Christians, education (or lack of it), family, home, relatives, friends, plus all of God's wonderful creation surrounding us.

A woman in one of my classes said to me, "I know I have these blessings, yet I have very little joy as a Christian. What's wrong with me?" As we talked together, I sensed that she probably did not know the meaning of Christ living in her, for joy is the result of His life in us. Happiness is the result of happenings, but joy is God's gift to us in Christ. (See John 15.)

Many of us are like this woman. We are subconsciously aware that we ought to be thankful for our blessings, but we have not yet made the decision that will bring God's joy to us.

We can have a full mature abundant life as believers or we can live in a wilderness. The choice is ours. The decision we make regarding the place Jesus Christ has in our life is going to completely change us—our thought patterns, our emotions, our temperament. We become new persons in Christ.

Jesus Christ is saying to us, "I want you to have these spiritual blessings which I have already prepared for you. I want you to mature in your knowledge of Me. I want you to know of Me, not merely to know about Me."

Let us pray these prayers of thanksgiving over and over, and the joy of His Presence will be given to us:

Thank You, Father, for every blessing I have—
   (name some) *my health, my family* (and others).
Thank You for Jesus in my heart.
Thank You that I belong to You and to Him.
(Use the list in the first paragraph of this devotional for additional subjects for thanksgiving.)

DAY 23

Read Ephesians 2.

For by grace are ye saved through faith; and that not of yourselves: it is the gift of God.
Ephesians 2:8, KJV.

How does one get faith?

Faith is a gift from God, given freely to all who ask. However, there is something we can do to build up our expectation and our faith, and that is to read the Bible. As we read of God's mighty works in delivering His children, and as we read the words of Jesus our Lord, faith is built up within our hearts. Faith to believe for our own salvation, for the salvation of our loved ones. Faith to believe in God's care and love, and His keeping power. Faith to believe that He can and will meet our personal needs in this life, and some day take us safely Home to be with Him forever.

Then there is the faith to believe for necessary miracles (answers to prayer) in everyday situations which need changing. Someone has said that "faith is the God-given ability to believe God for the impossible." By speaking words of faith, our own faith grows. By speaking words of faith, we help produce faith in others.

Keeping a notebook of answered prayer and of illustrations from actual life will encourage us to pray as we use them, repeat them to friends, and think on them. Fellowship with a small group of believers is vital to spiritual growth, for as we share together, faith grows, too, and where there is faith, there is answered prayer.

DAY 24

Read Ephesians 3:1–7.

I, Paul, the prisoner of Jesus Christ for you Gentiles . . .

Ephesians 3:1, KJV.

Paul had God's viewpoint toward his imprisonment. He could easily have said, "I, Paul, the prisoner of Nero." But though Paul was in Nero's prison he was not Nero's prisoner. He was the prisoner of Jesus Christ.

As two people examined a pearl oyster shell together, each saw it from a different viewpoint. One saw a black band running around the rim. The other saw a rainbow of color. Yet both were looking at the same shell, at the same time.

Viewpoint is important. The happenings of each day, all we encounter, can always be from two viewpoints. Do we see black or do we see a rainbow? Do we blame others (or circumstances) or do we see God's creative plan working for us? Do we see obstacles or opportunities? Our days on earth will always be lived out with limitations.

Lord, touch my eyes, so I can see things from your viewpoint.

DAY 25

Read Ephesians 3:8–21.

[asking] that you . . . be strengthened with power in the inner man, through His Spirit.
Ephesians 3:16, KJ II.

"What does 'power in the inner man' mean?" asked my friend Billie Mae. "How can I be strengthened; and is this the same as being *in Christ?*" I knew she wanted an answer in simple language which she could understand.

Let's take the last question first. My strength for the inner man comes from several sources—reading my Bible, feeding on the words of Jesus, praying in the Spirit, and meeting in fellowship with other Christians. As I am faithful in doing these things, I am instructed by the Holy Spirit and enabled to live the abundant life. Actually, this all can be summed up in a little prayer: *Lord Jesus, be Yourself in and through me.*

Being *in Christ* means that Christ is in me. I have fed upon this truth and know that I am only a branch and that He is the vine. Therefore, I repeat, because Christ is in me, I am in Him.

Now, let's take the phrase, "power in the inner man." Admission of weakness is the path to power. So I admit my insufficiency, my inadequacies, my selfishness. I know I am not always calm, loving, patient and kind, but I also know that Jesus Christ within me is all of these.

The union between us impels me to want to choose His will each day. He enables me to let Him be Himself through and in me. He is the power in my inner self. Christ in me always remains Himself. He never changes. And when I do, to my chagrin and sorrow, I simply ask forgiveness and take whatever responsibility I can to make things right. Then I leave it with Him and forget it.

Jesus Christ is the power within me to make me strong to follow Him and to do His will.

DAY 26

Read Ephesians 4.

If you are angry, don't sin by nursing your grudge. Don't let the sun go down with you still angry—get over it quickly.
Ephesians 4:26, LB.

"I'm always losing my temper," Sheila confided. "This frustrates my husband as he rarely loses his. I hate his smugness. I say and do things which he says he can't forget or forgive. I don't want a separation, but I need help. Please help me! How do I control my temper?"

These words came from the heart of an honest, fairly new Christian who had a real problem. Sheila took Ephesians 4:26 and began to live right in it. She prayed in it. She worked in it. She practiced it over and over again. And soon the power of honesty and prayer began to work her problem out. She shared with us how it was done.

"First, I was honest. I called temper and anger by their right names. They are sins, and I was guilty.

"Second, I did something about my temper tantrums before the sun went down, before I went to bed, like the verse says. I confessed it both to God and to my husband and asked their forgiveness. When I asked my husband to let me talk to him about what I did and why I was angry, he didn't want to listen to me—he'd had it! But God intervened, and finally we talked it out together. This helped me a lot.

"Third, I found it helped me to have my husband verbally tell me that he had forgiven me. I needed this. It took away my guilt feelings and my distress, and made me realize I never wanted to display my temper again.

"We were both surprised at the way the warmth, love and acceptance began to flood over us. I know this was God, and I gave Him the praise. All was forgiven and forgotten, and I felt loved and accepted from within.

"I am not totally over anger and temper, but I have come a long way. And I am confident that with God's help and my husband's love and consideration, I will have what I so desire—'the lasting charm of a gentle and quiet spirit which is so precious to God'" (1 Pet. 3:4, LB).

DAY 27

Read Ephesians 5:1-20.

Always give thanks for everything to God the Father, in the name of our Lord Jesus Christ.
Ephesians 5:20, TEV.

One woman says, "I am a housewife and without question I have the most uninteresting job in the world. My life is the same year in and year out—dishwashing, sweeping, dusting, cleaning, washing and ironing. I'm bored with myself, my family, and my friends. I'm discontented and unhappy and would like to be any place other than in this house."

Another woman says, "I am a housewife and without question I have the most fulfilling job in the world. My days are full of planning new things for our home, ways to make it more attractive. I plan for every member of our family to be happy, and want them to enjoy being at home. This is my calling and I am happy and content for this is the work which God has given to me."

What makes the difference between these two women? Their basic attitude. My question is, attitude toward whom? Certainly toward husband, family and home. But there is more to it than that. Notice that the second woman is happy and contented because she believes and knows that God Himself has called her to be a housewife. Therefore she can give thanks all day long, in season and out of season.

Here are some questions to help you sort out your basic attitude.

1. What is your attitude toward your husband? your family?

2. Does your attitude toward them show your attitude toward God?

3. What is your attitude toward God who loves you?

4. Think this one over: "We act our way into new ways of thinking, rather than think our way into new ways of acting" (Reuel Howe).

5. Wherever you are now, God is with you. Bloom where you are! This is today's slogan. Believe it and give thanks.

6. Read Ephesians 5:21–33 in *The Living Bible*.

DAY 28

Read Ephesians 5:21–33.

> *The wife must see to it that she deeply respects her husband—obeying, praising and honoring him.*
>
> Ephesians 5:33, LB.

My husband has wanted a new Cadillac for years. But whenever he brought up the idea, I always said, "All you ever do is drive back and forth to the office. What's wrong with your Chevy? Isn't it good enough for you?" Then he would drop the subject with, "Yes, I guess it is."

After much reading (and teaching others) on the subject of getting along with one's mate, I decided not to give my opinion the next time he asked. (I usually gave it whether I was asked or not.) I told myself I really didn't care if it was followed.

One day my husband came home and said, "I've joined the Golf Club." "That's great," I replied, "I'm glad you have." (I'd tried numerous times before to get him to do this.)

Then another day he said, "I want you to go to Bellevue with me and pick out a Cadillac. What color would you like?" I was delighted to go and forgot all about the Chevy, because I wanted him to be happy. He is a wonderful, responsible provider and deserves all the things he wants.

"Reverence your husband," the Apostle Paul said (see Eph. 5:33, Phillips). The implication is that I realize my husband's importance, and make him number one person in my life after my reverence for God. I am to be a help and not a hindrance to him. I am expected to fit into his plans, stay under his protection, and give him respect and honor. I have tried to do this and have been deeply rewarded to see that our son has the same attitude toward his father.

DAY 29

Read Ephesians 6.

Having done all . . . stand.
Ephesians 6:13, KJV.

"I have turned my problem over to the Lord, I have thanked Him for allowing me to have this problem, and I've thanked Him for the victory which I know He will give me. Now what shall I do?" How many times have you said this? You have a kind of peace, but at the same time you feel you should be doing something else, like discussing your situation with someone.

Paul's words are a command. When we've done all we can—have prayed, given thanks, trusted—we are just to stand still. While we are standing, we can remember how the Lord has worked for us in the past, and can open our eyes to see what He is doing now. Our tendency is to get so involved with what we want, that we do not see what God is doing.

We need to adopt the philosophy of taking things as they come. We should not suppose about tomorrow, or the results of today, but commit these entirely into His hands. We can learn to take the hard place without shock, without being upset, without resentment, when we recognize and believe that God is in control.

I have found that when I become irritated because of inactivity, if I just stop and take three deep breaths in and out, it helps me relax. Next, I can relax my body by lying down. It is very hard to be irritated lying down. (Try it for yourself. Let go of your muscle tensions—flop down any place you can.)

Sometimes I repeat the 23rd Psalm aloud, phrase by phrase, dwelling on each thought in positive affirmation.

Another verse I use, when I need to stand still, is Philippians 4:7: "The peace of God, which passeth all understanding" is now flooding my mind, my soul, my body. I repeat it over and over, until I feel the peace that only Jesus gives.

These procedures always relieve tension, stress, strain and nervousness for me. The peace of God is a gift to us through His beloved Son.

DAY 30

Read Psalm 37:1–11.

Commit thy way unto the Lord; trust also in him; and he shall bring it to pass.

Psalm 37:5, KJV.

What is the complaint you have this morning? What would make life easier or more livable for you? If you can pinpoint that complaint, you can commit it to the Lord, and trust Him to bring the answer.

Look over this list of heart-desires, and check the ones that trouble you, or plague you, or that make you feel insecure:

The circumstance you cannot control.

The person who has failed you.

The son or daughter who was dedicated to the Lord, but who is not interested at all in spiritual things.

The resentment you feel toward God because He withholds from you that which He gives to others.

The love you wish were in your home and is not.

That strong person whom you are stumbling over.

The husband who never expresses his love for you.

The great desire to pray with someone, a friend, your spouse, or as a family unit.

Now, in order to make your request more personal and more definite, write it out on a piece of paper. Hold it in your hands, and pray this prayer:

Lord, You said that if I would commit my way to You, and trust You, You would bring it to pass. I commit this ———— (name it) to You. I believe in Your loving kindness and tender mercy. I will sing praises to You and I will sing praises for the answer You are working out for me right now. I totally give this person (or problem) *to You right now. Glory be to the Father, and the Son, and the Holy Spirit. Amen.*

Third Month

DAY 1

> *Blessings on all who reverence and trust the Lord—on all who obey him!*
>
> *Their reward shall be prosperity and happiness. Your wife shall be contented in your home. And look at all those children! There they sit around the dinner table as vigorous and healthy as young olive trees.*
>
> *That is God's reward to those who reverence and trust Him.*
>
> *May the Lord continually bless you with heaven's blessings as well as with human joys. May you live to enjoy your grandchildren! And may God bless Israel!*
>
> *Psalm 128* LB.

Read this psalm aloud together as a family. Then, in turn, let each one thank God for every other member of the family by name. Verbally express love for and confidence in each other.

DAY 2

Read 1 Peter 3:8–22.

Be kind and humble with one another.
*Peter 3:*8q, TEV.

"Five o'clock is the 'witching' hour at our house. Kids are yelling; they are tired, dirty and cross. And I'm trying to get them cleaned up, fed, and ready for bed so their father and I can have our dinner in peace and quiet.

"It rarely turns out like I plan it. The house which had been straightened up is now a mess, the bathroom likewise, and I'm a mess too. I prefer to be beautifully groomed, rested and responsive when my husband gets home, but I am none of these.

"I would like to suggest we all go out for dinner, but it takes such elaborate arrangements for three children—aged five, three and two—that I stay home in self-defense. Finally, after one-half hour with their tired father, we are ready to dine alone. Do you know what happens? Arguments and disagreements on how to raise our kids! The privacy and spontaneity so desired are gone. We find we haven't much to say to each other, and the little time we do have together is wasted, when actually, that was the time we needed to forget self-pity and give comfort, understanding and love to each other. I feel I ought to receive love and understanding because I have been giving all day. But my husband feels he ought to be on the receiving end.

"So the big 'I' stands in our way."

Instead of being on the receiving end, why not try being on the giving end? Try giving to your children, and giving to your husband in love. Love makes your world a happy contented one even with all its problems.

You *can* love God together. You *can* communicate together. You *can* work at it. Then you will be ready to face anything together. As you grow in giving-love, you will find the real meaning of life which has eluded too many couples today.

I will always remember what Anna Mow said in one of her talks, "We are before God what we are in our families." This really shakes me, everytime I think about it. Why not think about that today, and talk about it this evening while you are dining together.

Rejoice and be joyful in your love toward God and each other.

"Be subject to one another out of reverence for Christ," (Eph. 5:21, NEB).

DAY 3

Read Proverbs 11.

Honor goes to kind and gracious women.

Proverbs 11:16, LB.

To be kind and gracious means to be sympathetic and full of love; to listen and understand. Women say to me, "I wish I had these qualities, but I don't. My family takes all my love, so how can I be gracious and kind to others when I can't perform in my own home?"

Have you ever thought about talking to God about the qualities you would like to have but never seem to find time to cultivate? Your heavenly Father loves to give good gifts like these to His children—even more than an earthly father would (Luke 11:9–13). Why don't you ask for what you need? Try it for a week or month, and watch God work in your life. Talk to God with expectancy, quoting this verse from Proverbs and trusting Him to remind you at that very moment to be kind or to be gracious. As soon as you see and hear your new behavior, you know He has heard you, so thank Him, and rejoice because He answered you.

A kind and gracious woman has time to sympathize with others. God actually returns to her the love and kindness she gives. As she shares with others, prays for them, believes for miracles for them, God gives her something special—honor and prestige.

Kindness and graciousness start right in your own home. Love and respect should be given to your own husband and to each child—not forgetting the middle one, who is so often unloved and neglected, or the handicapped one. As a wife, you are also mother and hostess: try your very best to make everyone *happy* that comes into your home; then expect God to make them good. He will.

Your task is custom-made for you—for a day, a week, a month—for always. *Be a kind and gracious lady.*

DAY 4

Read Proverbs 16.

> *We can make our plans, but the final outcome is in God's hands. . . . We should make plans—counting on God to direct us.*
> *Proverbs 16:1, 9,* LB.

We recently made plans for a trip to Greece and Turkey. But when we sent in our deposit, we were notified that we were on a waiting list. Right now there is exactly nothing else we can do about it. Waiting is not easy. Time slips by, other decisions have to be made, but they too must wait until this one is resolved. If the trip falls through, what then? It may mean someone else is to stay home so we can go, or it may mean we stay home and go on a later trip.

Am I, as a Christian, to get all steamed up about waiting? Throw our family into confusion? Badger the travel agency? No, definitely not. The Bible says I am to maintain "a gentle and quiet spirit" (1 Pet. 3:4, RSV), and be full of joy and praise.

This situation is one of the practical places that shows my Christianity is working. I have friends who are not believers, who are completely shaken because their plans are not working out.

We have placed our plans in God's hands. We trust Him with the outcome. We did all the necessary things. We prayed, we planned, we thanked Him for providing the means for the trip. Do I believe God cares about our plans? Yes, I do.

"Commit your way [this trip] unto the lord, trust also in Him, and He will bring it [the trip] to pass" (Ps. 37:5, KJ II). He did!

DAY 5

Read Proverbs 17.

Love forgets mistakes; nagging about them parts the best of friends.

Proverbs 17:9, LB.

How do you know when you are loved? Love forgets mistakes. It is human to forgive, but it is divine to forget, as Alexander Pope said. Only with God's help can any human being both forgive and forget.

So what if people do frustrate us and ruin our day? We need to make it a point to forgive them quickly, before the sun goes down. Because we are children of God, His grace will enable us to forget the incident entirely. God, who forgives us, gives us the power to forgive others.

God is saying to us now, "Come here, my child. I love you. I accept you. I forgive you. I have forgotten all your wrongdoings. I accept you right now, just as you are. Come here . . . to me . . . receive my love."*

We need to stop and give thanks for all our friends—the friends we can love, and forgive, and even forget their mistakes. God will bless us for doing this. Forgiving, forgetting and giving thanks cleanses our souls, and brings glory to God. Persistence in these three things will establish a pattern which can become a way of life. The day will come when we will discover that we are doing them quite unconsciously.

The main purpose of being a Christian is to learn to love one another as Christ loves us.

---

*Adapted from Rosalind Rinker's "Meditation No. 4" in *Communicating Love through Prayer*, Zondervan, 1966.

DAY 6

Read Proverbs 18.

The name of the Lord is a strong tower: the righteous runneth into it, and is safe.
Proverbs 18:10, KJV.

Today's message: Use the name of the Lord, the name of Jesus, to find comfort, security and protection.

In her book *Hind's Feet,* Hannah Hurnard's main character is a girl named Little Afraid. Her fear was that no one would ever love or accept her. At the Shepherd's bidding she started on a journey over the mountains alone, in search of love. While she had left behind the people and things that caused her fear, she found more things to be afraid of as she traveled.

Before she started out, the Good Shepherd told her she merely had to say His name, JESUS, and immediately He would be there with her, and she would not be afraid. She did this in times of danger, and found it true. She was safe anywhere, anytime, any place, because she called on His name.

You may have a great fear that is troubling you. Look up right now and say His name. Give your fear to Him, know He is there and you are safe. When the fear returns (and it may for a period), do not accept it. The name of Jesus is a prayer in itself, and you will be taken into His strong tower where nothing can touch you unless it first touches Him.

Memorize Proverbs 18:10, along with the "Jesus Prayer," and use them constantly.

The Jesus Prayer:

> *Lord Jesus Christ,*
> *Son of God,*
> *Have mercy on me.*

DAY 7

> *Ability to give wise advice satisfies like a good meal.*
> Proverbs 18:20, LB.

> *A wise man's words express deep streams of thought.*
> Proverbs 18:4, LB.

> *He who loves wisdom loves his own best interest and will be a success.*
> Proverbs 19:8, LB.

> *Humility and reverence for the Lord will make you both wise and honored.*
> Proverbs 15:33, LB.

> *If any man lacks wisdom let him ask it of God who gives freely and does not reproach. And it shall be given to him.*
> James 1:5, KJ II.

I have been told by women, "I haven't anything special to pray for today. What should I pray for? Any suggestions?" Well, why not ask for wisdom?

Today ask for wisdom in handling your home situation. Ask that you give wise advice to your teenagers. That your words will show you have thought the situation over from God's viewpoint. That you know what is for your best interest, that you give reverence to the Lord your God. In return He will honor you and give you the gift of wisdom.

Having asked for wisdom, expect it, look for it, seek for it with your whole heart. It might come to you through your smallest child, your neighbor, your husband, your church group. Or it might come from you. Just one experience of opening your mouth and hearing God's words flowing out of you like rivers of living water, changes your day and could change your entire life. The important thing is to recognize that it is God leading you into His wisdom.

If you lack wisdom, ask God for it!

DAY 8

Read Proverbs 27.

A man is tried by his praise.
Proverbs 27:21, ASV.

When people praise you, how does it affect you? Does it puff you up? Does it make you feel humble?

Do you want to offer the praise to your Lord or do you want to keep it for yourself? When God allows praise to be given to you, or conversely, withholds it from you, do you recognize your reactions?

If a man is tried by the way he takes his praise, he is equally tried by the way he takes blame. Do you make excuses? Do you want to retaliate? Do you place the blame on circumstances, or people?

Do you say, like Saul did to Samuel, "I have sinned: yet honour me now, I pray thee, before the elders of my people, and before Israel" (1 Sam. 15:30, KJV)?

Or do you say like David to God, "Against thee, thee only, have I sinned, and done this evil in thy sight" (Ps. 51:4, KJV)?

Our prayer in the face of praise and blame: *Lord, Jesus Christ, Son of God, forgive me and grant me your peace.*

DAY 9

Read Proverbs 29.

Where there is no vision, the people perish.
Proverbs 29:18, KJV.

My mother often quoted this verse to us when we were children. Later I learned she was really saying to us: "Without a vision of what you expect to accomplish and of what God wants your life to become, you won't amount to anything."

Without a vision I perish. This means that I must take time to be aware of and to enjoy God's creation. I need to see God in His creation—sky, water, clouds, trees, flowers, colors, animals. Most of all I need to see Him in His people. Looking for Him in the world around me will, in turn, open the windows of my heart and expose the flat surfaces of my mind, giving new dimensions to my little life. I will become a greater person.

Another vision that changes my life is the truth that God came into our world in Jesus Christ. When I believe on Jesus, He becomes my Savior and my Redeemer, reaching the deepest needs of my life. Today, the resurrected Jesus is the Holy Spirit teaching me what commitment means—that unless I die to my selfishness and pride, I cannot live a full and complete life.

One of the visions He has given me is that living for others brings more joy than living for myself.

For many years I couldn't see how the church had anything to do with my having a vision or perishing. But the longer I live the more I realize I need the church. I need the sacraments to remind me of the many mysteries in this present life—things I accept because they are part of life: birth, death, work, play, love, tragedy, illness, whatever. Also, I have come to understand that there is no perfect church. God's church is not a building at Sixth and Pine, but rather we who are His people are His true church. I am part of His church—you are part of His church—because He has said, "Wherever two or three come together in my name, I am there" (Matt. 18:18, 19, Phillips).

"All of you together are the one body of Christ and each one of you is a separate and necessary part of it" (1 Cor. 12:27, LB).

DAY 10

Read Proverbs 25:11–27.

A word fitly spoken is like apples of gold in pictures of silver.

Proverbs 25:11, KJV.

The telephone was ringing, and when I answered, a voice said, "I'm so relieved you're home. You have been on my mind and heart for days. Today I'm obeying that inner urge given to me by the Holy Spirit and I want you to know . . . I love you. You have been such a blessing to me. I'm sorry I waited until you were ill to tell you. I'm praying every day for your recovery, and I know you are going to get well. God has given me a promise for you: 'He spoke and they were all healed' " (Ps. 107:19, LB).

My caller kept talking, and though I couldn't get a word in, it was all right, for I was weeping. Yet my heart was full of thanksgiving and joy. This friend made the day beautiful for me and I was filled with love for everyone.

Hers were words "fitly spoken." I will never forget them. Words of encouragement are all too rare. We tend to think them rather than express them orally to each other.

Jesus speaks to you and to me, giving us golden apples in a silver basket (see Prov. 25:11 in *The Living Bible*) when we are lonely, discouraged, bereaved—or when we are happy and blessed. "I will never, *never* fail you nor forsake you" (Heb. 13:15, LB).

In your life today, who needs to hear words from you which will be like golden apples in a silver basket?

DAY 11

Read Philippians 1:1–11.

You are always in my heart! And so it is only right for me to feel this way about you.
　　　　　　　　Philippians 1:7, TEV.

You have a very special place in my heart.
　　　　　　　　Philippians 1:7, LB.

This week I said to my husband, "Thank you for your love and friendship. You are a sheer delight to me—a gift from God. I don't think I could have made it this past week without you."

I could see the instant happiness these words brought him. He even expressed it in words.

My husband wasn't the only one to whom I expressed my appreciation this week. I also told several people who are very special in my life what they mean to me.

I wanted to share this with you, because the warm relationship of one human being with another is one of life's greatest treasures. Expressing our intimate thoughts is not always easy, but it will bring someone great happiness. Isn't there someone in your family that needs to know they are a sheer delight to you?

Paul and the Philippians had this kind of relationship. In fact F. B. Meyer calls the Philippians "Paul's sweetheart church," because he tells them so often in his letter of his love and appreciation for what they are doing for him.

Thank You, Lord, for telling me that You love me.

DAY 12

Read Philippians 4:1–9.

Show a gentle attitude toward all.
Philippians 4:5, TEV.

Paul challenges the Philippians—and us—to show gentle love towards all.

When people fail me what do I do?

When people don't agree with me, what do I do?

When I can't stand being with some people, what do I do?

Paul gives me the answer. I am to "show a gentle spirit toward all." In other words, I need to be sweet, kind, reasonable; to have forgiveness and forbearance, and not to forget that the Lord is coming soon. I need to have that gentle spirit flowing out of me today!

I say, "Lord, I know I'm right and my neighbor is wrong." His answer: Be gentle with him.

I say, "I'm the big shot—he's just my helper. I don't like what he is doing." His answer: Be gentle.

I say, "He's taken advantage of me, so I can bless him or curse him." His answer: Be gentle with him.

Lord, give me a gentle attitude.
Let Your gentleness flow like a river in and out of me
*   . . . from You to me, and from me to others.*
Help me to remember You are coming soon.

DAY 13

Read Philippians 4:1–9.

Don't worry over anything, whatever; tell God every detail of your needs in earnest and thankful prayer, and the peace of God, which transcends human understanding, will keep constant guard over your hearts and minds as they rest in Christ Jesus.   *Philippians 4:6–7*, Phillips.

This verse tells us not to worry, but instead, to talk to God about every detail of our situation, in open, honest, and thankful prayer. The result is peace in our hearts and minds.

I had become very discouraged trying to sort out my anxieties and worries. I knew God could help me, but it seemed as though I was still relying on my own strength instead of His. All my attention was on that first clause, *don't worry about anything*. I said to my fretful self: Christ may be sitting on God's right hand in heaven, but it isn't doing me any good because I am still anxious.

Then one morning I felt impelled to read the entire verse again and as I did, the truth dawned on me. I needed to put my attention on the rest of that verse, not on that first clause. I needed all of the verse to make it work.

This is what I found: Tell God all about everything—even the details. Pray short prayers of thanksgiving for every problem and even for the solution (which He sees but which I am waiting for). The result follows like day follows night: His peace fills my mind and heart.

Lord, in my mind there are a crowd of little things pressing in on me. I am bringing them to You. I give them to You one by one (name them). *Remind me to keep the thanksgiving flowing for everything—good and bad—knowing that thanksgiving is the key to the peace of mind and heart which is Your gift to me. Then, all is well.*

DAY 14

Read Philippians 4:9–20.

But it was very good of you to help me in my troubles.

Philippians 4:14, TEV.

Getting involved, as the Philippian church became involved with Paul, means sharing another's joys and sorrows.

Getting involved means using my time to help
—the couple who can't get out
—the motorist who needs aid
—the girl who needs a job and a place to live
—the woman who gets ill while shopping
—the person who just found out she has cancer
—the person found weeping
—any person who is lonely or hurting.

I need to become involved with people in my church, in my neighborhood, in my city, in the whole wide world. And I need to start today with those whom I meet or know about.

DAY 15

Read 1 Thessalonians 5.

May our Lord pilot your hearts into the haven of the love of God, and into such calm patience as was Messiah's.
2 Thessalonians 3:5 (paraphrased).

Wonderful words of peace.

Words of calmness, of patience, of security.

Words of trust for those who put their hearts into the loving hands of God, not only for today but forever.

Only today is ours. Tomorrow is God's. Today the Lord is our pilot. He knows the way. He will guide our ship to the sure haven of His love, even if we don't know which direction we are headed.

Be assured, He knows.

He is faithful.

He is trustworthy.

He knows the unknown.

He will keep His hand upon the wheel.

The haven is His love and that is our resting place. A quiet harbor of acceptance, of unconditional, everlasting love.

Read the paraphrase at the head of this devotional several times. Then read this rendering of 2 Thessalonians 3:16 from *The Amplified Bible:*

"Now may the Lord of peace himself grant you His peace . . . at all times and in all ways—under all circumstances and conditions, whatever comes."

The quiet calmness which characterized our Lord will be ours, because we are His. The quiet calmness of our Lord is ours *right now,* because we are His.

St. Augustine said that all we have to do is to commit yesterday to God's mercy, today to God's love, and tomorrow to God's providence.

DAY 16

Read Jeremiah 33:1–3; Mark 9:14–29.

Call unto me, and I will answer thee, and shew thee great and mighty things, which thou knowest not.

Jeremiah 33:3, KJV.

If thou canst believe, all things are possible to him that believeth.

Mark 9:23, KJV.

Remember how the walls of Jericho fell? Under Joshua's leadership, the Israelites demonstrated that they believed God's promise by walking around the walls of Jericho for six days. But it was not until the seventh day that faith reached such a level that Joshua could say to the people, "Shout: for Jehovah has given you the city" (Joshua 6:16, ASV).

People often give premature declarations of faith which result in embarrassment. To avoid this and to let faith come to maturity, we must feed on God's Word until we are fully assured that what He has promised He will perform. God never, never mocks His children. You can bank on this one hundred percent.

We all need to encourage ourselves by reading God's Word. When you are experiencing a crisis and need an answer, if you will read the words of Jesus (what He has promised, what He can do) faith will be created within you.

"Faith comes by hearing and hearing by the Word of God" (Rom. 10:17, KJ II).

As you read and listen, the seed is sown in your heart; it is planted in your mind. Soon the harvest will come, and the answer will be yours. God actually says to you, "I will show you great things and difficult things, which you do not even know about" (Jer. 33:3, KJ II).

Believe and you will receive. Ask for great and difficult things, not just ordinary things. "Nothing is impossible with God."

At a camp meeting I attended when I was fifteen years old, we learned this chorus:

> Lord, I believe.
> Saviour, raise my faith in Thee
>   'till it can move a mountain.
> Lord, I believe. Lord, I believe.
> All my doubts are buried in the fountain.

DAY 17

Then said I, Ah Lord God!

Read Ezekiel 4.

Ezekiel 4:14, KJV.

Through a series of significant actions, the prophet Ezekiel was told to show the people of Israel what was going to happen to their nation. There was one thing so terrible that he asked God to excuse him.

"Ah Lord God!" he prayed, "spare me from doing this." God heard the prayer of one righteous man and reduced the pressure on an entire nation.

Have you ever felt that your little prayer didn't amount to very much? That God has so much work to do and such powerful things to take care of that He hasn't time for you? I did, until I memorized James 5:-16 and made it part of my life. "The effectual fervent prayer of a righteous man has much power with God."

There are times when we feel we can't cope with the situation, or that certain demands are beyond our power to endure. This is when we need to go into our closets, close the door, get on our knees and pray. "Oh, Lord God, have mercy on me. Oh, my Father, hear my prayer." Praying like this affirms our belonging to His family, helps to give us assurance that because He loves us He will hear and answer.

God wants us to be open and honest with Him. He wants us to say what we feel. "Oh, Lord God, I did this crazy thing. I'm in a mess and I know it was my fault. Help me out of this confusion. I'm a proud, egotistical person. I can't control my emotions toward a certain person."

Or, your complaint may be something like this: "Oh, Lord God, I don't like the way I feel toward You. I don't like the way You've been treating me. I feel so unimportant to You, and I guess I resent You. I feel rebellious toward You for what has happened to me."

There is health and healing in this kind of prayer language—in just talking your heart out. As you vocalize your feelings about God and about people, you are beginning to learn to know God better, and to know yourself better. This is good therapy. You are on your way to becoming a complete person—a temple of the Holy Spirit.

Don't be afraid to say, "Oh, Lord God, have mercy on me!"

DAY 18

Read Romans 8:26–39.

And we know that all that happens to us is working for our good if we love God and are fitting into his plans.

Romans 8:28, LB.

One morning I was driving into Seattle to buy a dress. Having neglected my Quiet Time before I left home, I started to pray while driving that I would get the right clerk, find the right dress, and not waste my time or anyone else's. While I was thinking and praying, I heard a siren and wondered if it was the police or the ambulance. But I gave it no further thought until suddenly I became aware that I was being stopped.

"Do you know you were going over the speed limit?" the policeman said with stern authority. "No, I wasn't aware of it," I replied. He snapped back, "How come you didn't know?" "I was praying about my shopping. I have to buy a dress and I was concerned about it."

"Madam," he replied, "you know you can be so heavenly minded that you are no earthly good. You live here, not There, so watch it, or you might live There sooner than you think." I admitted I was wrong and he was right, and I was lucky to receive only a warning ticket.

As I drove on, I felt some guilt but instead of turning the car around and going back home, I decided to pray about that experience. The guilt soon left me (I think because I admitted it to the officer and to my Father above). Then I prayed for that officer, because all unconsciously I had witnessed to him.

Thinking about the incident later, I began to blame the officer! Then I blamed myself, knowing I was ten miles over the speed limit and deserved a ticket. I was guilty, and felt guilty. But having acknowledged my wrong to the officer, and then to God, I began to see things clearly. When I turned to Him and sent up a flash-prayer for help, the circumstances altered, and

God gave me a thankful heart to praise Him for His care over me.

God is the engineer for all our circumstances. This old world provides all of us with enough rough places to get hurt. Blaming others or one's self is not the answer. Believing that all things do work together for good, *is* the answer, for it is God's way of showing His love for us.

DAY 19

Read Titus 2.

> *These older women must train the younger women to live quietly, to love their husbands and their children.*
>
> *Titus 2:4,* LB.

The best way to influence another is by personal example. As we live quietly, giving and showing love in our own families, that difficult person who is always coming to us for advice will want her home to be just like ours.

I speak at many women's conferences, and constantly some mother takes me aside and tells me, "I have a problem. I can't love one of my children. I am continually picking at him. I sometimes wish he weren't mine."

I heard this recently from a mother with two boys and a girl. She was speaking of her second son. I asked her, "Do you realize God loves Keith as much as he loves you? Do you ever pray with him?"

"No, I don't; he has asked me to but I tell him I'm too busy. I tell him, 'Say your own prayers and go to sleep.'"

Knowing how much love God could give her for that son, I said, "Some day, Sally, you will give everything you own to be able to pray with this son, to be able to tell him you love him, to have him love you. He senses now that you do not love him, that he is pushed aside, and that you prefer the other two children." "Yes," she replied, "I know he does."

I took her hands in mine and prayed for a new touch of God's love to fill Sally for her eight-year-old son, for Jesus to help her so she would be able to pray with him.

I suggested this prayer: "Lord Jesus, thank you for Keith. I know you love him. I love him too. Help us to show our love to each other. Keith is precious to you, and you have given him to me. Thank you again for my dear son. I love him. Amen."

As Sally and I prayed together, God touched her heart and love was born anew. Keith will respond sooner or later with his own prayer.

Later I learned that through prayer, Sally and Keith were brought together in love and understanding. The grandmother told me that she had prayed with her grandson and given him special love. She had been aware of the situation and had been praying about it, but not until Sally took the above action did the healing miracle take place.

God, help us to be kind and patient and loving toward our children. "For of such is the kingdom of heaven."

DAY 20

Read Hosea 1:1–2; 2:1–23.

Then you will lie down in peace and safety, unafraid; and I will bind you to me forever with chains of righteousness and justice and love and mercy.   *Hosea 2:18–19,* LB.

When God said these words to Hosea, you can imagine the comfort they were to him, after all the suffering he had experienced because of his erring wife.

"Hosea, I am going to look after you with right-ness, with justice; you can lie down and be in peace and not be afraid, for I love you and I am with you."

This message tells us a lot about what God is like. (When I first became a Christian, I kept a notebook as I read my Bible and wrote down all that I found about what God is like. This helped me to understand and to know Him better. It also gave me great comfort and security.)

Because Hosea went through very hectic times he has been called "the prophet of Israel's zero hour." He saw his people (of the northern kingdom, Israel) taken into captivity by the heathen nation Assyria. God did not give Israel another prophet after Hosea. (There were, however, other prophets to the southern kingdom of Judah after Hosea). He was God's chosen man for his generation. His book is written mainly in poetry. Read all of it sometime to see what God had to say to His people.

Would you like to have God use you? Would you like to be God's woman for your generation? You can be, for God is no respecter of persons. Like Hosea, turn to God when you have a difficult situation in your home. Read His Word, let Him talk to you, listen to the still small voice.

He could be saying to you, "Mary (or whatever your name is), I am going to look after you because I care about you. I care about what has happened, and what is happening right now. You do not need to be lonely nor afraid, for I am with you. I will never leave you nor forsake you. You are my very own. You are precious in my sight."

DAY 21

Read Hosea 14.

I will heal their faithlessness;
I will love them freely,
for my anger has turned from them.
I will be as the dew to Israel.

Hosea 14:4–5, RSV.

When the northern kingdom was troubled by political instability and the threat of invasion by foreign powers, the Israelites did not turn to God and say, "What have we done, Lord, to deserve this treatment? We need help. We need your justice, mercy, love and forgiveness."

What did they do instead? They turned to other heathen nations for help and alliance. They chose to trust in men rather than in God.

Hosea called his people to turn to God, to seek help from Him and follow His ways. Today some Christians turn to the signs of the zodiac, to fortune-tellers, palm-readers, and unbelievers. Then, as a last resort, they turn to God.

God said to Israel, "If you will turn to me and love me, I will be your God and you will be my very own people. I will bind you to me forever." But they were so far away from Him that they did not even hear His words.

Your personal worry may not be as vast as Hosea's concern with the state of Israel. But you can still follow Hosea's prescription and turn to God. Write your problem, your worry, your situation on a piece of paper. Cup your hands together and put the paper in them. Now say to God, "Dear Lord, I can't face this alone. It troubles me continually and hinders me in serving You. Right now I give it totally and unconditionally into Your hands. It is Your concern now and I give praise for Your plan for me."

As you finish, drop the paper on the floor and put your feet on it, or drop it into a wastebasket, or burn it.

Then audibly, begin to thank and praise God for His answer. Every time it comes back into your mind, continue with praise and thanksgiving. Remember "X" marks the spot, the time and the place where you gave it to Him. You never, never have to take it back into yourself again.

Then you can lie down in peace and safety as Hosea did, and feel God's comfort, His chains of rightness, justice, mercy and love binding you to Him.

For He does all things well (Mark 7:37).

DAY 22

Read James 1

> *Dear brothers, don't ever forget that it is best to listen much, speak little. . . .*
> *James 1:19*, LB.

I am usually so busy living that I do not take time to listen to the Lord.

Does this sound familiar to you: *If I hadn't been so preoccupied I would have heard You, Lord.*

The Virgin Mary listened and heard all the angel had to say to her. She never forgot a single word. Even during the thirty long years before the ministry of Jesus began, she remembered what the angel told her. When almost everyone was questioning Jesus' authority, she did not. She remembered. She had listened. Later, she told it all to St. Luke, and he wrote it down for us to read in the early chapters of his Gospel.

Lord, teach me to listen, to remember and to obey.

DAY 23

Read James 5:13–20.

Confess your faults one to another, and pray one for another, that ye may be healed.

James 5:16, KJV.

Virginia was a member of our prayer and Bible study group. She had an unhappy face, and listened to the rest of us share our problems and pray together for six months before she opened her own heart.

In this group of dedicated women, we speak very personally about our relationship with Jesus. We practice honesty and acceptance of ourselves and of each other. We do not try to judge one another, or to make each other over. Only God can make us what He wants us to be.

The day finally came when Virginia came out with the deep need which was hurting her. "I can't stand it any longer, I need help, too. I hate the place I live in!"

Three of us immediately surrounded her, and touched her in love, as we prayed—that this very week God would change things for her, that she might come to accept the fact that God had a purpose in putting her in that house. Then we all gave thanks, thus accepting the answer to our prayers for her.

You should have seen us the following week when our group met! We were all lined up waiting for Virginia to arrive, after praying for her that entire week. She came in with her face aglow, and almost in unison we started giving thanks to God, for the change in her. It broke up our meeting!

This was the first time Virginia had ever opened her heart. Since then she has grown in faith and love because she took the risk and shared her problem. Sharing in a group is the way healing comes to many of us. The whole group was filled with the same joy Virginia received, as God's love flowed through our hearts in thanksgiving.

DAY 24

Read 1 Peter 1.

Be ye holy; for I am holy. 1 Peter 1:16, KJV.

God means just exactly what He says. He is holy and He expects you and me to be holy. This is a command, not a suggestion or a request.

Have you ever asked yourself how God can expect you to be holy when you are an imperfect human being? In a letter I received recently, a friend expressed her dilemma: "I am very mixed up about this being holy, because I am so full of self. I try to study and read about God, but I can't seem to get into the rhythm of walking with God. Sometimes my prayers bring release and peace and sometimes they don't. How can I ever be holy in His sight?"

God who commanded us to be holy will give us, as a gift, His righteousness (which is holiness) through His Son, Jesus Christ. (Read 1 Cor. 1:30.) He does not command us to *feel* holy, but to accept the holiness of Christ and to walk in obedience; not looking at ourselves, but being willing to admit daily when we have failed. (See 1 John 1:7.) When failure comes, that's you, not He.

How do you start? Choose to accept this holy God into your life, to believe on Him, love Him, and obey Him. This God is Jesus Christ. Put your mind on Him. Learn of Him.

Forget yourself. Stop worrying about being holy, because your quiet trust in His life new within you will produce this fruit. When the heart (or root) is occupied by Jesus Christ, the thought life, emotions, conversation, actions, attitudes (the branches) will be like Him.

What a miracle it is that God makes us holy without making us self-righteous. How can you know if you are self-righteous? Try asking your husband or your best friend. They probably will be glad to have the opportunity to express themselves on the subject.

God, who makes you holy, will help you to show His holiness to others without being self-righteous. Remember, Jesus Christ within you, is your righteousness (1 Cor. 1:30).

DAY 25

Read 1 Peter 3:1–6.

When they observe the pure and modest way in which you conduct yourselves, together with your reverence [for your husband. That is, you are to feel for him all that reverence includes]—to respect, defer to, revere him; [revere means] to honor, esteem (appreciate, prize), and [in the human sense] adore him; [and adore means] to admire, praise, be devoted to, deeply love and enjoy [your husband].

1 Peter 3:2, Amplified.

Dear Mrs. Adler: This verse saved my marriage. It also saved the lives of my husband and three children. We didn't have weeds; we had hay, stubble and garbage to plow through!

My husband is an alcoholic and abused all of us, so I took over the establishment and made all the decisions. I lost all respect, honor and esteem for my husband. Before I knew it, my children had, too. They learned it from me.

Attending your classes, we studied 1 Peter 3:2, and you suggested we take this verse seriously and act on it.

Well, I did. It took six long months. I praised my husband for everything he did around the house, for his pay check, even though short. I gave him consideration and love, and went out of my way to make him comfortable, to give him prestige and guidance.

I suggested that the children ask him for direction when he was home. I referred to him as head of our family. I told him how enjoyable his company was—even though it was in front of the TV.

Our kids thought I'd flipped, but my husband responded with sympathy, understanding, and finally, love. The first time in years he came home Christmas Eve with an arm full of gifts and his whole paycheck.

Isn't Jesus wonderful? I can't thank Him enough!

                        Sincerely in His love,

                              Helga

P.S. He says he will attend church with the family next Sunday. I will keep you posted.

P.S. (By Denise) Three months later he was baptized upon confession of faith and joined the Lutheran church.

DAY 26

Read 1 Peter 3:7–22.

You should be like one big happy family, full of sympathy toward each other, loving one another with tender hearts and humble minds.

1 Peter 3:8, LB.

Do you give your husband genuine love and admiration? Or do you just respect him? I hear this statement over and over, "I respect my husband but I do not love him." Or, "I love my husband but I do not respect or admire him."

Let me ask you a few questions. Do you know what is actually in your husband's heart? Do you know what he thinks about? What he dreams about? Do you get him to talk about himself, his hopes, his ambitions?

You may say, "He doesn't do any of these things for me, why should I listen to him? I'm too busy with the children, with his house, etc., etc."

That's not the point. Right now we are talking about husbands, and yours in particular. If you listen to him, draw him out, share with him, you will begin to admire him. Without admiration your husband becomes a lonely man and will seek out others who will give this to him. The more admiration you give, the more love you receive.

Your son also needs admiration in order to develop confidence in himself. This works with every member of your family, as well as your in-laws.

Let's look at some of the things you can do. 1. Set out to discover in your husband qualities you have overlooked. 2. Take a vital interest in him; give yourself and give him appreciation (remember, if you don't, someone else will). Learn to listen to him. Often he will talk just to gain your admiration. If you enjoy listening, he may be inclined to help you with your work, the dishes, or grocery shopping, or tending the kids.

Believe it! Your husband has physical, spiritual, and mental traits you can admire. Find these, build up his ego, praise him, thank God for him (verbally). Praise him for his guidance, protection and support for you and the children. Never take him for granted. You set the example, you take the lead, and the children will follow.

Peter tells us to win our husband by our example, not by our talking.

DAY 27

Read Habakkuk 1:1–2:4.

I will climb my watchtower now, and wait to see what answer God will give to my complaint.

Habakkuk 2:1, LB.

How many complaints do you have stacked up in your mind? Do you think you are the only one who has them? More than two thousand years ago God's prophet, Habakkuk, felt alone with many complaints. What did he do? He climbed up into his watchtower where He knew God would speak to him.

Your watchtower is your place of meditation! A chair, a bed, a table, a window, a garden—any place where you can go to talk to God. You may say, "I'd like to tell God my complaints, but if I do, I'll feel guilty." Just voice them anyway; say them aloud or write them down. For one thing, objectivity is good therapy; for another, it will make you realize Someone *is* there and that He cares about you.

For instance, you could say:
Lord, don't You care about me?
I'm dying by inches, don't You care?
I'm nothing but a servant. Nobody in my family appreciates me.
I'm hurting. I want to tell You about myself.
I don't like what I'm doing.
Lord, You aren't answering any of my prayers.
It takes You so long, Lord, and I'm in a hurry!

Habakkuk poured out his complaints and then said, "Lord, what answer will You give me?" The Lord said, "Wait, watch and write down what I tell you."

God said much more to comfort him, but here is my own paraphrase of what God told him (from Habakkuk 2:1–4):

"As you are waiting for Me to work things out, set a watch over what you do and say today. The things I plan for you will not happen right away. The answer may seem to be slow, but do not despair, for these things will surely come to pass. Be patient, they will not be overdue a single day.

"While you are waiting for My answers, go about your regular work as usual, but be aware that I am working and that the answer is coming."

DAY 28

Read Zechariah 7:8–14.

Then this message from the Lord came to Zechariah. "Tell them to be . . . merciful and kind to everyone."

Zechariah 7:8–9, LB.

Although these words come from the Book of Zechariah (about 500 B.C.), let us remember that God's truth is the same today as it was yesterday. So the word of God to us is to be merciful and kind to everyone we meet today.

You say, "I try to be kind to everyone I know." God is saying that that is not enough. You have to be specific. Kindness to everyone means that we need to dig down to that one person whom we cannot love.

A woman from our Bible class said to me once about another woman, "I can forgive her for what she did to me, but I can't forget it. I really don't like her. How can I love her as long as I am remembering what she did to me?"

My husband and I found an answer to that question. A certain woman caused my husband great anguish in his business. We could forgive her, but we were unable to forget the anguish. Then we started to pray together for her. We set a goal of praying for five minutes the first day; however, after one short minute, we found we had both said our little prayer and were through! The next day we could pray a bit longer, then for five minutes, and then even more. Finally we could give this woman our love. And when we did that, the hurt was gone; we had forgotten.

How can you be merciful and kind to the one who wounds you? Jesus is saying, "Come to me and receive my love and my forgiveness. As I give these to you, you will be able to give them to another. You will still have the memory, but I will take the pain away and give you forgiving love in its place."

"This commandment have we from him, That he

who loveth God love his brother also" (1 John 4:21, KJV).

Exercise:
 Visualize the person you can't forgive.
 Surround him with God's love and yours.
 Pray for him five minutes every day for one week.
 If you chance to meet him, give him this love through your voice and your eyes.

DAY 29

Read 1 John 3:1–18.

See how very much our heavenly Father loves us . . .

1 John 3:1, LB.

If you have difficulty praying, it could be that you really do not believe God loves you . . . you, personally. When you can't pray, just be quiet, and listen and wait.

I recall a time when I couldn't find words to pray. This went on for days until I realized I had to do something to restore the communication between my Lord and me. I stumbled onto the truth (but God led me to it, I learned afterwards) that I didn't believe God really loved me—as a person, as I was. I didn't love myself, so how could I blame God for not loving me! In fact, why should He bother about me, when He had the whole world on His hands?

Finally, in desperation I wrote the words *Jesus loves me* on several recipe cards and put them on my dressing table, and on my sink. For one week, everytime my eye fell on one of the cards I repeated the words as a prayer. Then the next week I made another set of cards: *I love Jesus.* I said those words to Him for a full week. The next week I linked them together: *Jesus loves me and I love Jesus.*

By that time, these positive affirmations had thoroughly "brainwashed" me with God's truth, and I believed it with all my heart.

Negative ideas did arise to kick me about, with such thoughts as, "How simple can you get! You, with a master's degree, and you have to say three or six words for three weeks!" But it worked, and that is the proof of the pudding.

Since that time I have never doubted His personal love for me nor mine for Him. Best of all, I can pass His love on with confidence because God made a miracle in my life with three little words.

He can make a miracle in your life too.

DAY 30

Read Revelation 8.

Then another angel with a golden censer came and stood at the altar; and a great quantity of incense was given to him to mix with the prayers of God's people, to offer upon the golden altar before the throne. And the perfume . . . ascended up to God from the altar where the angel had poured them out.

Revelation 8:3-4, LB.

My mother used to thank God for the sweet smelling incense of the Christian's prayers which came up before God. Since she has gone home to be with the Lord, I have understood more of what she was talking about. It really was not until I learned the joy of talking with God through the power of the Holy Spirit, that I began to see how prayers could be fragrant like perfume.

There have been times when I'm half ashamed to bring some things to my Lord, but I have come to see that all prayer is like incense and is dear to the heart of God. In fact, it is so precious to Him, the writer of Revelation pictures it as being brought to Him in a golden censer by an angel who offers it up on a golden altar.

So let us come boldly with our requests, our daily needs, our prayers for others. Let us remember that they are being offered as fragrant perfume in the presence of our Lord.

"Let my prayer be counted as incense before thee, and the lifting up of my hands as an evening sacrifice!" (Ps. 141:2, RSV).

DAY 31

Read Hebrews 12:1–4.

Consider him that endured . . . lest ye be wearied and faint in your minds.
Hebrews 12:3, KJV.

What an uplift these words bring! We look at ourselves and are defeated. We look at others and are not helped. But when we look at Him who endured, we are marvelously lifted up. We are no longer weary or faint in our minds. Love and strength come through as we look at Him. He is our Lord, our beloved Lord. He makes the difference. Then we can endure with joy and be done with faint hearts.

During the years I was teaching school before I was married, I was often extremely tired after a long, hard day. I'd come home and want to go right to bed without eating or talking to anyone. Then the telephone would ring and it would be Lloyd, my beloved, suggesting that we go out to dinner. You know my answer. I would "consider him" and instantly the weariness and tiredness would be gone and I would be up, dressed, and gone in fifteen minutes.

This is the way it happens when we consider our living, loving Lord.

The good word is "Consider Him."